Youth

Strength

Training

A Guide for

Fitness

Professionals

from the

American

Council

on Exercise®

By Avery D. Faigenbaum, Ed.D.,
and Wayne L. Westcott, Ph.D.

ABCDE

ISBN: 1-58518-924-3
Library of Congress Control Number: 2004117528

Distributed by:
American Council on Exercise
P.O. Box 910449
San Diego, CA 92191-0449
(858) 279-8227
(858) 279-8064 (FAX)
www.ACEfitness.org

Managing Editor: Daniel J. Green
Technical Editor: Cedric X. Bryant, Ph.D.
Design & Production: Karen McGuire
Director of Publications: Christine J. Ekeroth
Assistant Editor: Jennifer Schiffer
Index: Bonny McLaughlin
Models: Andrew DeLacey, Timmy Leung,
Jeremiah Rohner, Katelyn Sidley,
Randall D. Walker, Jr.
Cover models: Andrew DeLacey,
Jennifer DeLacey, Lisa DeLacey, Timmy Leung
Photography: Dennis Dal Covey
Cover Photograph: Jamie Robinson

Acknowledgments:
Thanks to the entire American Council on Exercise staff for their support and guidance
through the process of creating this manual.

*Special thanks to Hoist Fitness Systems for providing the facilities and equipment for the
exercises shown in Chapter 4.*

NOTICE
The fitness industry is ever-changing. As new research and clinical experience broaden our knowledge,
changes in programming and standards are required. The authors and the publisher of this work have
checked with sources believed to be reliable in their efforts to provide information that is complete and
generally in accord with the standards accepted at the time of publication. However, in view of the
possibility of human error or changes in industry standards, neither the authors nor the publisher nor
any other party who has been involved in the preparation or publication of this work warrants that the
information contained herein is in every respect accurate or complete, and they are not responsible for
any errors or omissions or the results obtained from the use of such information. Readers are encouraged to confirm the information contained herein with other sources.

Published by:
Healthy Learning Books & Videos
P.O. Box 1828
Monterey, CA 93942
(888) 229-5745
(831) 372-6075 (Fax)
www.healthylearning.com

LONELY BRANCH

Introduction

Nearly a century ago, in a society where most workers performed physical labor, there were relatively few adults who needed auxiliary strength-building workouts and almost no one trained with weights. Farmers, for example, performed various forms of resistance exercise for much of the day, most days of the year. Children were also more fit, as they performed plenty of chores and pursued physically active pastimes. In an era without television, computers, video games, or fear of playing outside, youth enjoyed lots of vigorous exercise, including relatively long walks to and from school.

Unfortunately, boys and girls of the 21st century have much more sedentary lifestyles, with little time or opportunity for regular physical activity apart from organized sports. Few children walk to school, physical education is rapidly becoming a thing of the past, and the continuation rate in organized sports decreases dramatically beginning in early adolescence. In many cities and suburban areas, parents are afraid to let their sons and daughters play outside without adult supervision. It is truly a tough time to encourage American youth to engage in regular physical activity, and children are paying large consequences for their sedentary behavior.

Coincident with the epidemic of childhood obesity, many preadolescents have preliminary markers of heart disease, osteoporosis, and type 2 diabetes, not to mention weak muscles and low levels of physical fitness. This is not a pretty picture, but there is hope on the horizon.

Interestingly, youth will not thrive when following the typical adult model of aerobic activity, characterized by five minutes of warm-up treadmill walking, 30 minutes of steady-state treadmill walking at 70% of maximum heart rate, and five minutes of cool-down treadmill walking. In fact, the vast majority of preadolescents simply will not adhere to this type of exercise protocol. It is a totally unnatural activity pattern for children who typically exercise hard for about a minute, then rest briefly before exercising hard for another minute, and so on. In addition, most research shows that young children have a limited ability to increase their cardiovascular fitness by performing standard aerobic-activity programs (Zwiren, 2001). Continuous endurance exercise is not particularly effective or enjoyable for preadolescents, but they seem to thrive with stop-and-go activities that have sufficient recovery periods between successive short bouts of exercise.

The physical activity that best fits the previous description is strength training, defined as the use of progressive resistance exercises (e.g., using weight machines, free weights, elastic tubing, medicine balls, bodyweight) to increase children's musculoskeletal health and fitness. Essentially all standard protocols of strength exercise require about a minute of exertion (10 to 15 repetitions of one exercise), followed by one to two minutes of rest before performing another minute of muscular exertion (10 to 15 repetitions of another exercise).

Consider also that overweight youngsters do not run, jump, or maneuver well on playing fields. In fact, they do not even like to play tag games because they are typically the first ones caught or eliminated. However, heavier youth tend to be able to lift heavier weights than their lighter counterparts, which makes strength training a most appropriate and appealing physical activity for them. For once, they can participate in an exercise program at the same or even higher level than their peers, which really reinforces their training efforts. Strength training is the perfect physical activity for building a strong musculoskeletal system in overweight boys and girls, and is equally important for all youth.

Some people mistakenly believe that strength training is a dangerous activity for preadolescents. There is not a single reported incidence of any serious injury in all of the prospective studies ever published on youth strength training. And in our more than 20 years of work in youth strength training, no child has experienced an exercise-related injury. Clearly, supervised strength exercise is an extremely safe form of physical activity for young people, and one that has proved effective for increasing both bone mineral density and musculoskeletal fitness in preadolescents.

This book addresses the research-based recommendations for safe, sensible, effective, and efficient youth strength training, and presents practical guidelines for successfully implementing strength-building programs for preadolescent boys and girls. In addition to clear instructions and illustrations of strength exercises using youth-sized resistance machines, adult-sized resistance machines, free-weight equipment, elastic bands, bodyweight resistance, and medicine balls, we provide sample workouts using each of these training modalities.

Although anyone interested in youth strength training will benefit by reading this book, it is especially designed for fitness instructors, with an entire chapter devoted to teaching tools and program design. We hope that you will enjoy reading and implementing the information presented in these pages as much as we enjoyed consolidating our youth strength training research studies and compiling the most important concepts into book form.

Avery Faigenbaum, Ed.D.
Wayne Westcott, Ph.D.

Introduction to Youth Strength Training

Strength training is recognized as a safe and effective method of exercise for adults, and a growing number of children are strength training to improve their health and fitness as well. Although aerobic activities such as swimming and biking are typically recommended for children, a compelling body of evidence indicates that strength training can be added to the list of physical activities that boys and girls can perform safely and benefi- cially. Despite traditional concerns associated with this type of exercise, all major fitness and medical organi- zations in the United States now recommend strength exercise for youth provided that appropriate training guidelines are followed. Moreover, public health objectives discussed in the *Surgeon General's Report on Physical Activity and Health* aim to increase the number of youth aged six and older who regularly participate in physical activities that enhance and maintain muscular strength and endurance (U.S. Department of Health and Human Services, 1996).

Youth fitness classes that include strength training are now offered at schools and fitness centers, and many youth coaches are incorporating strength and conditioning exercises into the workout plans for their young athletes. Yet misconceptions about youth strength training still persist and some professionals remain uncertain about recommending this type of training for preadolescents. Furthermore, parents often inquire if their children can "lift weights" and fitness instructors are often asked to provide information on appropriate strength-training guidelines for boys and girls.

Misconceptions and Facts

Answers to questions and concerns regarding the safety and effectiveness of youth strength training should be based on a current review of the scientific literature and not case study reports or anecdotal information. Here are responses to some of the most prevalent misconceptions about youth strength training.

Misconception. Strength training may stunt the growth of children.

Fact. This misconception seems to have been fueled by a report from the 1960s that suggested children who performed heavy labor were short in stature (Kato & Ishiko, 1964). However, other causative factors such as poor nutrition or very long work days were not controlled in this study. No evidence indicates that regular participation in a well-designed strength-training program will stunt the growth of children. Although strength training will not make a child taller, regular participation in a strength-training program may actually increase the bone strength of children and, therefore, decrease their risk for developing osteoporosis later in life.

Misconception. Children cannot increase their strength because they do not have enough testosterone.

Fact. Although testosterone enhances muscle size and strength development, high levels of testosterone are not essential for achieving strength gains. This is evidenced by the fact that children, women, and elderly individuals can make impressive gains in strength even though they have very little testosterone. While children may have a more difficult time increasing muscle size in response to strength training as compared to older populations, relative (i.e., percent) strength gains observed in children are comparable to adults.

Misconception. Children should not lift weights until they are 12 years old.

Fact. Children can begin strength training when they have the emotional maturity to accept and follow directions. In most cases, if a child is ready to play a sport, then he or she is ready to strength train. As a point of reference, hundreds of seven- and eight-year-old boys and girls have participated in youth strength training programs at the South Shore YMCA in Quincy, Massachusetts.

Misconception. Children will get "big and bulky" from strength training.

Fact. Training-induced strength gains during childhood are primarily due to neural adaptations rather than an increase in muscle size. Children will not get "big and bulky" from strength training, but will become better at recruiting and coordinating muscle fibers when performing an exercise.

Misconception. Strength training is only for young football players.

Fact. Young athletes in all sports, including soccer, basketball, swimming, and tennis, can benefit from strength training. Although the demands of each sport are different, both general and sport-specific strength-training programs can enhance muscle strength, local muscular endurance, sprint speed, and jumping ability. In addition, young athletes who strength train are better prepared for sports competition and may be less prone to injury.

Misconception. Bodyweight exercises such as push-ups and pull-ups are safer for children than exercises using weight machines or free weights.

Fact. Although some people believe that bodyweight exercises are safer for children, no evidence supports this claim. Different modes of strength training, including weight machines, free weights, and bodyweight exercises, have proved equally safe and effective for youth provided that qualified instruction is available and age-specific training guidelines are followed. Furthermore, attempting a pull-up or even a push-up often requires a maximal exertion from a sedentary or overweight child. In such cases, it

may be safer and far more enjoyable for the child to perform strength-building exercises on a weight machine or with dumbbells using a load that is consistent with the child's current muscular ability.

Potential Benefits

Along with sports and other recreational activities, appropriate strength-training programs can offer observable health and fitness value for boys and girls. In addition to enhancing muscular fitness, youth strength training has the potential to positively influence many other indices of health and fitness. Regular participation in a youth strength-training program may increase bone mineral density, facilitate weight control, positively impact selected psychosocial measures, enhance motor performance skills, and increase young athletes' resistance to sports-related injuries. A summary of potential health and fitness benefits associated with youth strength training is presented in Table 1.1.

Table 1.1
Potential Health and Fitness Benefits of Youth Strength Training

- Enhanced muscular fitness
- Increased bone mineral density
- Improved body composition
- Improved motor fitness performance
- Enhanced sports performance
- Increased resistance to injury
- Enhanced psychosocial well-being
- Improved attitude towards lifelong physical activity

Health-related Benefits

Available research indicates that the health of children is more likely to improve than be adversely affected by regular participation in a strength-training program. In fact, many of the health benefits associated with adult strength-training programs are attainable by preadolescents who follow age-specific training guidelines. Although additional research is needed to fully elucidate the effects of strength training on children's health, instructors who work with youth should appreciate the potential positive impact of strength training on a child's well-being and functional capacity.

Outdated concerns that strength training would damage the growth plates of children or stunt the growth of boys and girls have been replaced with reports suggesting that childhood may be the optimal time for bone-modeling processes to respond to the progressive muscle loading of strength-training activities. Growth plate fractures have not been reported in any prospective youth strength-training study and observations indicate no evidence of a decreased stature in children who regularly train with weights. If children are taught how to strength train properly and if sound nutritional recommendations are followed (e.g., adequate calcium), strength training will likely have a favorable influence on bone growth and development.

Although peak bone mass is strongly influenced by genetics, strength training has proved to be a promising intervention for enhancing bone mass in children. This potential health benefit may be particularly important for girls, who are at increased risk for developing osteoporosis later in life. As we get older, the prevention of skeletal frailty depends not only on reducing bone loss during adulthood, but also on maximizing bone mass during childhood. Since osteoporosis is a major public health problem, encourage children to engage in appropriate weightbearing and muscle-loading activities on a regular basis.

Another potential health benefit of youth strength training is its influence on body composition. As the number of overweight children in the United States continues to rise, the beneficial effects of strength training on body composition have received increased attention. Although aerobic exercise is often recommended for decreasing body fat, several studies have reported significant decreases in body fat in youth following regular participation in a strength-training program (Faigenbaum et al., 1993; Lillegard et al., 1997).

Although the treatment of childhood obesity is complex, observations suggest that overweight children enjoy strength training because it is not aerobically taxing and it gives all participants—regardless of body size—the opportunity to experience success and feel good about their performance. Since overweight youth tend to be the strongest in class, they often receive unsolicited positive feedback from their peers who are impressed with the amount of weight they can lift. Unlike prolonged periods of aerobic exercise in which most overweight youth "fail," strength training gives overweight boys and girls a chance to gain confidence in their physical abilities. It seems that the first step in encouraging overweight children to exercise may be to increase their confidence through successful strength-training experiences, which in turn may lead to an increase in regular physical activity.

Perhaps the most overlooked benefit of youth strength training is its potential impact on psychosocial health (i.e., psychological and social outcomes). If the training program is well-designed and if the instructors are aware of the physical and psychological uniqueness of youth, strength training may offer psychosocial benefits that are comparable to other recreational activities and sports. Significant improvements in general self-esteem have been observed in youth following a strength-training program (Holloway et al., 1988), and the socialization and mental discipline exhibited by youth who strength train are similar to youth participating in team sports (Faigenbaum, 1995). While all youth can benefit from strength training, it seems that strength training may have its greatest impact on children and adolescents who begin with relatively low levels of muscular fitness and poor body images.

Parents and youth coaches have also reported that well-designed strength-training programs may positively influence children's attitudes toward physical education, physical fitness, and lifelong exercise. However, it should be noted that excessive pressure from parents, coaches, and instructors to perform at a level beyond one's capabilities can negatively influence the youth strength-training experience and can lead to adverse psychosocial consequences.

Motor Performance Skills and Sports Performance

One of the most recognized benefits of youth strength training is its impact on motor performance skills. Strength training has been shown to improve many skill-related components of physical fitness, including speed, power, agility, and coordination. Several reports have noted significant improvements in the long jump, vertical jump, sprint speed, and agility run time following participation in a youth strength-training program (Lillegard et al., 1997; Weltman et al., 1986; Williams, 1991). And since these skills are important for success in sports, one can only assume that a stronger and more powerful athlete will perform better.

Although observations from parents and coaches suggest that strength training enhances athletic ability, scientific reports supporting this finding are limited because athletic ability is influenced by so many different factors, such as genetics, coaching, experience, and lifestyle habits (e.g., good nutrition and adequate sleep). Nevertheless, it appears that strength training will likely result in some degree of improvement in sports performance by enhancing a young athlete's muscular fitness and general well-being.

Sports Injury Reduction

Well-designed youth strength-training programs can also help to reduce sports-related injuries in young athletes. While millions of youth participate in sports in the United States, it seems that a growing number of boys and girls are ill-prepared for the demands of sports practice and competition. Unfortunately, few children participate in physical education on most days of the week and some youth spend more than 20 hours per week in front of the television or computer screen. Although many factors, such as training errors (e.g., too much too soon), hard playing surfaces, and improper footwear, have been implicated as potential risk factors for overuse injuries in young athletes, the background level of physical activity must also be considered.

By strength training, aspiring young athletes can improve the strength and integrity of their muscles, tendons, ligaments, and bones, and develop muscle balance around joints, which may decrease the incidence of injuries. Several research studies have demonstrated lower injury rates in teenagers who participated in a preseason conditioning program that included strength training, and it seems likely that preadolescents would experience similar benefits if appropriate training guidelines are followed. This type of conditioning may not only better prepare young

athletes for sports practice and competition, but it may even decrease the likelihood of drop-out due to embarrassment, failure, or injury. Some clinicians believe that up to 50% of overuse injuries in youth sports could be prevented if young athletes were better prepared and conditioned to play the game.

Although the total elimination of sports-related injuries is an unrealistic goal, it seems prudent for boys and girls to participate in at least six weeks of preparatory conditioning (including strength, aerobic, flexibility, and agility training) before sports participation. During this time, correctable risk factors such as poor physical condition can be identified and treated by qualified instructors. The bottom line is that a youngster's participation in physical activity should not start with sport competition, but should evolve out of preparatory conditioning that includes strength training. In some cases, young athletes may need to decrease the amount of time they spend practicing sport-specific skills to allow time for conditioning exercises that strengthen their musculoskeletal system.

Basic Guidelines

It is important to encourage children to be physically active for at least 30 to 60 minutes on most days of the week as part of play, games, school, or work. Not only do physical activity habits established during childhood tend to track into adulthood, but a physically active lifestyle early in life may also help to prevent some chronic diseases later in life. While a variety of physical activities should be recommended for youth, this section will discuss basic guidelines for developing a youth strength-training program.

Although there is no minimum age for participation in a youth strength-training program, all participants should have the emotional maturity to accept and follow directions and should understand the benefits and risks associated with strength training. Furthermore, children who want to participate in strength-training activities should receive guidance and instruction from a qualified instructor who understands strength-training principles and genuinely appreciates the physical and psychological uniqueness of childhood.

No matter how big or strong a child is, adult training philosophies should not be imposed on young weight trainers. Instructors should listen to concerns and closely monitor each participant's ability to handle the exercise stress. When introducing youth to strength-training activities, it is always better to underestimate their physical abilities rather than overestimate their physical abilities and risk an injury. While it is important to gradually increase the weight, the number of repetitions, or the number of sets over time, this does not mean that every exercise session needs to be more intense than the previous session. Children should be given the opportunity to develop proper form and technique with minimal

muscle soreness on a variety of exercises before progressing to higher levels of training.

Although some youth may want to see how much weight they can lift during the first training session, their energy and enthusiasm for strength training should be directed toward developing proper form and technique on a variety of exercises with a submaximal weight. Teaching youth about proper exercise technique and safe strength-training procedures, such as controlled movements and proper breathing, are important considerations. Remember, it is always easier to master the technique of an exercise the first time than try to break bad habits and "relearn" how to perform an exercise properly the second time.

Attempting to lift a heavy weight during the first week of the program may be particularly harmful for youth because it not only increases the risk for injury, but it may also undermine the enjoyment of the strength-training experience. Even though tangible outcomes such as an increase in muscle strength are important, when working with children it is important to focus on other factors such as skill improvement, personal successes, and having fun, which are the primary reasons youth participate in physical-activity programs.

Because children do not develop the capacity for abstract thought and reason until ages 11 to 14, they are unable to delay gratification in pursuit of some future benefit like strong bones. Therefore, youth should be encouraged to embrace self-improvement and feel good about their own accomplishments. Abstract thinking begins to emerge by the upper elementary school years, at which time children are more likely to be motivated by improvements in health and may be more willing to tolerate more structured strength-training programs.

Instruction and Supervision

Unsupervised and poorly performed strength exercises may be injurious to children. Always be aware of the inherent risks associated with strength training and attempt to decrease this risk by following established training guidelines. Children should never strength train on their own without guidance from a qualified instructor who clearly explains and properly demonstrates all exercises. Enforce safety rules; unsafe behavior in the training area must not be tolerated under any circumstances. If you recommend home-based strength-training programs (especially if free weights are used), ensure that children will be supervised by a competent adult and that appropriate training loads are used.

Summary

Despite previously held beliefs that strength training was ineffective or unsafe for youth, a compelling body of evidence indicates that children can benefit from regular participation in a strength-training program. Provided that the training program is appropriately designed and competently supervised, youth strength training may enhance the health and fitness of boys and girls. An understanding of strength-training principles and safety procedures is essential, and should provide an opportunity for all children to have fun and feel good about their successes.

Strength-training Fundamentals

CHAPTER TWO

A wide variety of health and fitness benefits can be expected from regular participation in strength-building activities, provided that fundamental training principles are followed. Fundamental strength-training principles are described below, along with program-design considerations that can be used to safely and effectively enhance muscular fitness in children.

Fundamental Training Principles

While numerous strength-training programs may increase muscle strength, adherence to fundamental training principles is mandatory to maximize the benefits of strength training. Although factors such as the initial level of fitness, genetics, nutritional status, and motivation will influence the rate and magnitude of adaptations that take place, three fundamental concepts related to the effectiveness of all strength-training programs are the principles of progressive overload, exercise specificity, and program variation.

Progressive Overload

The principle of progressive overload has been a basic tenet of strength training for more than a century. This principle states that to continually make gains in muscular fitness, the body must exercise at a level beyond its normal stress level. For example, a child who can easily complete 10 repetitions with 20 pounds while performing the chest press exercise should increase the weight, the repetitions, or the number of sets if he wants to make additional gains in upper-body strength. Otherwise, if the training stimulus is not increased, training adaptations will not occur. Thus, a gradual increase in training "overload" is required for long-term gains in muscular fitness.

It is important to individualize the exercise program and pay particular attention to the magnitude of progression. A general guideline is to increase the training weight by about 5 to 10% and decrease the repetitions by two to five when a given load can be performed for the desired number of repetitions with proper exercise technique. For example, if a child can easily complete 15 repetitions while performing a leg press exercise using 100 pounds, she should increase the weight to 105 pounds and decrease the number of repetitions accordingly (e.g., 10 repetitions) if she wants to continually make gains in muscle strength. Alternatively, she could increase the number of sets, increase the number of repetitions, or add another leg exercise to her exercise routine.

Exercise Specificity

The principle of exercise specificity refers to the distinct adaptations that take place as a result of the strength-training program. This principle is often referred to as the SAID principle (Specific Adaptations to Imposed Demands). In essence, every muscle or muscle group must be trained to make gains in strength, power, and/or local muscular endurance. For example, exercises such as the leg press and leg curl can be used to enhance lower-body strength, but these exercises will not affect upper-body strength.

Moreover, adaptations that take place in a muscle or muscle group will be as simple or as complex as the stress placed on them. Single-joint exercises such as the dumbbell biceps curl are relatively simple to perform, whereas multijoint exercises such as the medicine ball squat are relatively complex and require more balance and coordination to execute properly. Since most sports and activities of daily life require complex multijoint movements, the principle of exercise specificity can be applied to the design of strength-training programs for youth who want to enhance their sports performance as well as their ability to perform activities of daily life.

Program Variation

The principle of program variation refers to systematically altering the strength-training program over time to allow for the training stimulus to remain optimal. Performing the same workout over and over again is not only boring, but over time it also becomes ineffective. The principle of program variation is sometimes referred to as periodization and is used to achieve specific goals, avoid overtraining, and keep the program effective and challenging. In recent years, the principle of program variation has received increased attention and our factual understanding of the potential benefits of changing the training program over time has increased.

Periodically varying the strength-training program by changing the choice of exercise or the combination of sets and repetitions can optimize gains in muscle performance. For example, if a child's upper-body routine typically consists of the chest press and seated row weight machines, performing the dumbbell chest press and dumbbell row on alternate workout days will likely add to the effectiveness and enjoyment of

the strength-training program. Furthermore, varying the number of sets and repetitions can help to prevent training "plateaus," which are not uncommon in youth fitness programs. There is no single strength-training program that will work for all children; therefore, it is important to remember the general concept of program variation, which is to prioritize training goals and then develop a long-term training program that varies throughout the year.

Health and Safety

A youth strength-training program should be based on a child's health history, current fitness level, and individual goals. Develop safe and effective strength-training programs by assessing the needs of each participant and applying basic training principles to the program design. However, because the magnitude of adaptation to a given exercise stimulus varies among individuals, it is prudent to be aware of individual differences and be prepared to change the program to reduce the risk of injury and optimize strength gains.

Health and Fitness Status

Parents or legal guardians should complete a health-history questionnaire for each child prior to participation. The questionnaire should ask about pre-existing medical ailments (e.g., asthma, diabetes), recent surgery, allergies, and previous musculoskeletal injuries. While it is not mandatory for apparently healthy children to have a medical examination prior to strength training, the health questionnaire can help identify youth with known or suspected health problems who should be screened by their physician or healthcare provider prior to participating in a physical activity program.

Additional questions on the pre-participation health-screening questionnaire regarding past strength-training experiences, sport involvement, and activity interests can also aid in the design of the strength-training program. Children who have the least experience with strength training tend to have a greater capacity for improvement when compared to more experienced lifters. For example, a 12-year-old with two years of strength-training experience may not achieve the same strength gains in a given period of time as a 10-year-old who has no experience with strength training. This is based on the observation that the potential for adaptation gradually decreases as training experience increases.

Safety Checklist

Before designing youth strength-training programs, be sure you are knowledgeable of safe and effective training methods and understand the physical and psychological uniqueness of children. While all strength-training activities have some degree of medical risk, you can reduce the risk of injury by following established training guidelines and safety procedures.

Always be able to teach correct form for the exercises you recommend, and be able to make modifications in exercise form and technique if necessary. Also, know the exercises that require spotters and be prepared to offer assistance in case of a failed repetition. When working in a school, community center, or fitness facility, be attentive and try to position yourself with a clear view of the training center so that you can have quick access to children who need assistance. In addition, you are responsible for enforcing safety rules (e.g., proper footwear, safe storage of weights, no "horseplay" in the fitness center) and safe training procedures (e.g., emphasizing proper exercise technique rather than the amount of weight lifted). Table 2.1 presents general safety recommendations for designing and instructing youth strength-training programs.

Table 2.1
Safety Recommendations

- Provide qualified supervision and instruction.
- Review each child's health history before the program begins.
- Maintain a safe and clutter-free training environment.
- Ensure that children understand the benefits and risks of strength training.
- Participate in warm-up and cool-down activities.
- Use collars on all plate-loaded barbells and dumbbells.
- Follow proper spotting procedures when needed.
- Periodically check all strength-training equipment.
- Do not allow "horseplay" in the weight room.
- Encourage children to stay hydrated before, during, and after class.
- Have an emergency plan in place in case of a serious accident.
- Keep accurate records of all training sessions.

Leadership Characteristics

Before working with children you must have an understanding of strength-training guidelines and safety procedures. Speak with children in a language they understand and discuss the potential benefits and risks associated with this type of training. Always relate to children in a positive manner and realize that some may need additional time and instruction to master the performance of an exercise. Moreover, match the strength-training program to the needs, interests, and abilities of each participant. A structured strength-training program for a high school athlete would be inappropriate for a preadolescent who should be given the opportunity to experience the mere enjoyment of strength training in a non-competitive environment.

In some cases, instructors who are wonderful with adults may lack the patience, enthusiasm, and understanding to work with children. Staff training sessions and continuing education seminars can help you develop the skills needed to work with youth effectively (Table 2.2).

Facilities and Equipment

The strength-training area of a public, community, or school-based fitness center should be well-lit and large enough to handle the number of boys and girls exercising in the facility at any given time.

Table 2.2
Tips for Youth Fitness Instructors
- Greet every child by name when they arrive at your program.
- Listen to concerns from all children.
- Focus on skill improvement, personal successes, and having fun.
- Adapt the program to the child's developmental level.
- Increase the resistance gradually and progressively.
- Provide feedback in a positive and constructive manner.
- Incorporate variety into the training program.
- Thank participants for coming to your program.
- Be a good role model and lead a healthy lifestyle.

Keep the facility clean and the equipment well-maintained. Equipment pads that come in contact with the skin should be cleaned daily, and cables, guide rods, and chains on machines should be checked weekly. Space equipment adequately to allow easy access to each strength-training exercise, and return free weights and collars to the proper storage area after each use.

Activity-related accidents can usually be prevented if safety is made a priority. Take a few minutes before every class to ensure that the training environment is safe and, if necessary, remove or disassemble any broken pieces of equipment from the exercise area. Keep in mind that overcrowded exercise areas increase the chance that a child may get hurt or bump into another participant.

Modes of Training

Different modes of strength training can be used to accommodate the needs of children. Provided that the fundamental principles of training are adhered to, almost any mode of strength training can be used to enhance muscular fitness. Some types of equipment are relatively easy to use and others require balance and coordination. A decision to use a certain type of mode of strength training should be based on each child's needs, goals, and abilities.

The major modes of strength training are weight machines, free weights (barbells and dumbbells), bodyweight exercises, and a broadly defined category of medicine balls and elastic tubing. Table 2.3 summarizes the advantages and disadvantages of different modes of strength training.

While some youth can use adult-size weight machines, child-sized weight machines are now manufactured by several companies and are designed to fit the smaller body frames of children. Both single-joint (e.g., leg extension) and multijoint (e.g., leg press) exercises can be performed on weight machines, which are relatively easy to use because the exercise motion is controlled by the machine. This is particularly important to consider when designing strength-training programs for sedentary or overweight youth who typically lack confidence in their fitness abilities.

Free weights are also popular in youth fitness centers and come in a variety of shapes and sizes. While it may take a little longer to master proper exercise technique using free weights compared to weight machines, there are several advantages to free-weight training. For example, proper fit is not an issue when using adjustable barbells and dumbbells because "one size fits all." Free weights also offer a greater variety of exercises than weight machines because they can be moved in many different directions.

Another important benefit of using free weights is that they require the use of additional stabilizing and assisting muscles to hold the correct body position while performing an exercise. This is particularly true when using dumbbells because they train

Table 2.3
Comparison of Different Modes of Strength Training

	Weight Machines	Free Weights	Bodyweight	Balls & Tubing
Cost	High	Low	None	Very low
Portability	Limited	Variable	Excellent	Excellent
Ease of Use	Excellent	Variable	Variable	Variable
Variety	Limited	Excellent	Excellent	Excellent
Space needs	High	Variable	Low	Variable

each side of the body independently. However, unlike weight machines, several free-weight exercises require the aid of a spotter who can assist the lifter in case of a failed repetition. The use of a spotter is particularly important on the bench press exercise to help ensure safe exercise participation.

Bodyweight exercises such as push-ups, pull-ups, and curl-ups are some of the oldest modes of strength training. Obviously, a major advantage of bodyweight training is that little or no equipment is needed and a variety of exercises can be performed. Conversely, a limitation of bodyweight training is the difficulty in adjusting the resistance to the strength level of the individual. Sedentary or overweight youth may not be strong enough to perform even one repetition of a push-up or pull-up. In such cases, bodyweight exercises may have a negative effect on program compliance. Exercise machines are available that allow individuals to perform bodyweight exercises such as pull-ups and dips using a predetermined percentage of their weight. These machines provide an opportunity for participants of all abilities to incorporate bodyweight exercises into their strength-training program and feel good about their accomplishments.

Medicine balls and elastic tubing can be also be used in youth strength-training programs. Medicine balls and elastic tubes come in different sizes and levels of resistance and can be a safe and effective alternative to free weights and weight machines. For example, children can squat while holding a medicine ball or perform a chest press with an elastic tube. Not only are medicine balls and elastic tubing relatively inexpensive, but they also can be used to enhance strength and local muscular endurance. In addition, some medicine ball exercises such as the chest pass can be performed explosively. This type of fast-speed training can add a new dimension to a workout, which can be particularly beneficial for young athletes who need to develop strength and power.

Summary

Children who want to start strength training should seek guidance from qualified instructors and adhere to fundamental training principles. Pre-screen youth for medical conditions that warrant medical referral and educate them about the benefits and concerns associated with strength training. While different modes of strength training can be effective, the design of the strength-training program will influence the training-induced adaptations that occur. Qualified instruction, a safe training environment, and adherence to established training guidelines will help to minimize the risk of injury, optimize training adaptations, and encourage a lifelong interest in strength training.

Strength-training Guidelines

CHAPTER THREE

The following guidelines for safe, effective, efficient, and enjoyable youth strength-training protocols are based on 25 years of experience working with youth and researching youth fitness. The majority of this research has examined standard strength-training variables such as frequency, resistance, repetitions, and sets.

Exercise Selection

There are many considerations for selecting appropriate resistance exercises for youth strength-training programs, including facility space, equipment availability, participant age, training objectives, and instructor abilities.

For example, a circuit of single-station weight-stack machines requires more facility space than does a single multistation apparatus, a set of dumbbells, or medicine balls. Along the same line, a circuit of single-station weight-stack machines provides a fixed number of exercises, whereas dumbbells, elastic bands, and medicine balls allow for considerable variation in exercise selection.

Although boys and girls from ages seven to 15 can safely participate in all forms of sensible strength training, the supportive structure, inherent stability, and fixed movement patterns of well-designed resistance machines are preferable for younger children, especially during introductory training programs. Training objectives also influence exercise selection. While exercises using machines and free-weights are ideal for developing overall muscle strength, they should be performed at relatively slow movement speeds. On the other hand, power development may be enhanced by using relatively fast movement speeds with medicine balls.

Of course, you must be competent and confident in the proper use of the selected equipment and exercises. Whereas most instructors are comfortable teaching machine exercises, others lack the knowledge and experience necessary for effectively teaching and supervising free-weight and medicine-ball training.

Regardless of the type of equipment, utilize approximately eight to 12 basic exercise movements that cumulatively address all of the major muscle groups. This may be accomplished by using multiple-muscle linear exercises (e.g., leg press, chest press), single-muscle rotary exercises (e.g., leg extension, biceps curl), or a combination of linear and rotary exercises. Bodyweight exercises may also be incorporated into the exercise options, especially for the important core muscles (i.e., erector spinae, abdominals, obliques) that may be effectively trained with trunk curls, trunk extensions, knee-lifts, and related movements.

If youth-sized resistance machines are available, we suggest the following strength exercises, categorized according to the major muscle groups they address (Table 3.1).

Although younger children will not fit properly on adult-sized rotary machines (e.g., leg curl, lateral raise), they can typically use adult-sized linear machines (e.g., shoulder press, seated row) as long as the starting weights are not too heavy for proper exercise performance.

Recommended free-weight exercises are presented in Table 3.2. Of course, different dumbbell and/or barbell movements can be

Table 3.1
Recommend Machine Exercises for the Major Muscle Groups

Muscle Group	Primary Exercise	Additional Exercise
Quadriceps	Leg press	Leg extension
Hamstrings	Leg press	Leg curl
Gluteals	Leg press	
Pectoralis major	Chest press	Chest cross
Latissimus dorsi	Seated row	Pull-down
Deltoids	Shoulder press	Lateral raise
Biceps	Arm curl	Weight assist chin-up
Triceps	Arm extension	Weight assist dip
Rectus abdominis	Modified trunk curl	Knee lift
Erector spinae	Birddog	

substituted, but these represent a basic circuit of age-appropriate free-weight exercises.

For the most part, dumbbell exercises can be successfully performed with elastic resistance. Likewise, medicine balls can be used for a variety of movements such as chest presses, shoulder presses, and lunges. The major advantage of medicine ball training is the ability to release the resistance, thereby allowing faster movement speeds for greater power production. For example, underhand medicine ball throws involve the quadriceps, hamstrings, gluteals, erector spinae, deltoid, upper trapezius, and biceps muscles in sequential, accelerated actions.

Table 3.2
Recommended Free-weight Exercises for the Major Muscle Groups

Muscle Group	Primary Exercise	Additional Exercise	Alternative Exercise
Quadriceps	DB Squat	DB Step-up	MB Lunge
Hamstrings	DB Squat	DB Step-up	DB Lunge
Gluteals	DB Squat	DB Step-up	DB Lunge
Pectoralis major	DB Bench press	DB Incline press	DB Chest fly
Latissimus dorsi	DB Bent-over row	DB Pull-over	MB Pull-over
Deltoids	DB Shoulder press	DB Lateral raise	DB Upright row
Biceps	DB Arm curl	BB Arm Curl	Weight assist chin-up
Triceps	DB Standing extension	MB Standing extension	Weight assist dip
Rectus abdominis	Trunk curl	MB Abdominal curl	
Erector spinae	Trunk extension		

DB = Dumbbell Exercise   **BB = Barbell Exercise**   **MB = Medicine Ball Exercise**

Frequency

Research with adults reveals that beginning exercisers achieve excellent results training three, two, or one day a week, with somewhat less benefit at the reduced exercise frequencies—when compared to three weekly exercise sessions, subjects attained about 85% as much muscle gain from training twice a week and about 70% as much muscle gain from training once a week (Westcott, 2000). On the other hand, essentially the same muscle strength improvements can be experienced by boys and girls who train either three or two days a week.

To reduce the risk of boredom or burnout in young people who have lots of other activities in their daily routines (e.g., school, homework, instrument practice, sports participation, boy scouts, religious education, computer time, television time, reading time, pet care, household chores, paper route, family events), two strength-training sessions per week, on non-consecutive days, is a general recommendation.

Research has shown that children between seven and 12 years of age who train one day a week achieve only 67% as much strength gain as those who perform identical workouts two days a week (Faigenbaum et al., 2002). Twice-a-week strength training for youth appears to provide both better physiological results and program continuity, especially considering that children may need additional recovery time between successive training sessions due to growth and maturation processes.

One exception to this guideline is in-season youth athletes who are doing large amounts of vigorous physical activity. A study of 10-year-old female figure skaters concluded that one weekly strength workout during their competitive season produced significant improvement in the subjects' body composition, upper- and lower-body strength, and jumping performance (Westcott, 2000). Additionally, the girls were pleased with their strength-training program, as the single weekly exercise session complemented rather than complicated their relatively full schedule of skating practice and competition.

Resistance

The heaviest weightload that can be lifted with proper form for one repetition is considered an individual's maximum resistance, or 1 RM weightload. For most practical purposes, adults train between 60 and 90% of their 1 RM weightload. Because children are not necessarily miniature adults, they should train in the lower half of this resistance range (60 to 75% of 1 RM). Although reports of injuries in supervised youth strength-training programs are rare, the use of moderate weightloads should further reduce the risk of injury or overtraining.

Rather than regularly evaluating the children's 1 RM, estimate their training resistance based on the number of exercise repetitions they can complete with correct technique. Most people can perform about 10 good repetitions with 75% of their 1 RM weightload and approximately 15 repetitions with 60% of their 1 RM weightload. Young people should begin strength training with a resistance they can lift for 10 to 15 properly performed repetitions.

Children who train with heavier weightloads (75 to 90% of 1 RM) actually attain less improvement in muscle strength and muscle endurance than those who train with lighter weightloads (60 to 75% of 1 RM) (Faigenbaum et al., 1999). Apparently, performing more repetitions with lighter weightloads provides greater motor learning stimulation and neuromuscular facilitation for enhanced strength development.

Repetitions

As previously indicated, exercisers can perform more exercise repetitions with lighter weightloads and fewer exercise repetitions with heavier weightloads. This basic relationship is presented in Table 3.3.

It is generally assumed that low-repetition training is preferable for increasing muscle strength and that high-repetition training is preferable for increasing muscle endurance. However, this does not appear to be the case when working with preadolescent boys and girls. Elementary school children (mean age 8 years) demonstrate significantly greater gains in both muscle strength and muscle endurance when training with higher (13 to 15) repetitions

Table 3.3
Percent of the 1 RM and Repetitions Performed

Percentage 1 RM	Number of Repetitions Performed
100	1
95	2
93	3
90	4
87	5
85	6
83	7
80	8
77	9
75	10
70	11
67	12
65	15

Adapted, by permission, from Baechle, T.R., Earle, R.W., & Wathen, D. (2000). Resistance training, In: *Essentials of Strength Training and Conditioning* (2nd ed.). NSCA, edited by T.R. Baechel & R.W. Earle. Champaign, Ill.: Human Kinetics.

than when training with lower (6 to 8) repetitions (Faigenbaum et al., 1999). As shown in Table 3.4, these findings are consistent for upper- and lower-body exercises.

Other studies have also demonstrated greater strength development from higher-repetition training (10 to 15 reps) than from lower-repetition training (six reps) (Faigenbaum et al., 1993; 1996b). Based on these findings, it is recommended that youth start strength training with exercise sets of 10 to 15 repetitions. While they can train safely and effectively with lower repetition ranges, this exercise protocol appears to be more productive for improving muscle strength and muscle endurance, particularly during the first several weeks of training.

Table 3.4
Effects of Youth Strength Training Using Higher Repetitions and Lower Weightloads versus Using Lower Repetitions and Higher Weightloads (N=43).

Variable	Control Group (No Exercise)	Low-rep Group (6 to 8 Reps)	High-rep Group (13 to 15 Reps)
Leg extension Strength gain	+13.6%	+31.0%	+40.9%
Chest press Strength gain	+4.2%	+5.3%	+16.3%
Leg extension Endurance gain	+3.7 Reps	+8.7 Reps	+13.1 Reps
Chest press Endurance gain	+1.7 Reps	+3.1 Reps	+5.2 Reps

Sets

Research with adults indicates that both single-set and multiple-set training promote strength gains, with some studies favoring multiple sets and other studies showing no significant differences in strength development. The best results reported in the youth strength-training literature were attained using a three-set protocol developed by DeLorme and Watkins, in which the first set is performed with a light resistance, the second set is performed with a medium resistance, and the third set is completed with a heavy resistance (Faigenbaum et al., 1993). The weightloads for each set are based on the heaviest resistance that can be completed for 10 good repetitions (Table 3.5).

The DeLorme-Watkins program permits progression to a new 10 RM weightload only when the present 10 RM weightload can be performed for 15 good repetitions (DeLorme & Watkins, 1948). Although this workout protocol requires a longer training session than single-set programs, it has proven highly productive in research studies. As presented in Table 3.6, 10-year-old boys and girls who followed the DeLorme-Watkins program increased their overall

Table 3.5
Sample DeLorme-Watkins Three-set Strength-training Protocols Based on the Participant's 10-Repetition Maximum Weightload

Participant's Present 10 RM Weightload	First Set: 50% of 10 RM Weightload	Second Set: 75% of 10 RM Weightload	Third Set: 100% of 10 RM Weightload
100 lb	50 lb	75 lb	100 lb
80 lb	40 lb	60 lb	80 lb
60 lb	30 lb	45 lb	60 lb

Table 3.6

Changes in Muscle Strength for Youth who Performed Eight Weeks of Resistance Exercise According to the DeLorme-Watkins Training Protocol (23 subjects, mean age 10 years)

10 RM Strength (In Kilograms)	Exercise Group (N=14)			Control Group (N=9)		
	PRE	POST	%CHANGE	PRE	POST	%CHANGE
Leg extension	12.9	21.2	64.5*	12.1	13.8	14.1
Leg curl	10.4	18.5	77.6*	12.0	13.6	13.2
Chest press	15.2	25.0	64.1*	13.4	15.0	12.5
Overhead press	7.5	14.1	87.0*	7.8	8.8	13.1
Biceps curl	4.7	8.3	78.1*	4.8	5.3	12.2
Mean % change			*74.3*			*13.0*

Note: *=statistically significant change ($p<.05$)

muscle strength by almost 75% after eight weeks of twice-a-week strength training.

It is interesting to note that the first two sets in the DeLorme-Watkins protocol are relatively easy warm-up sets that progressively prepare the exerciser for the personally challenging and physiologically stimulating training set. The two preliminary sets appear to facilitate the neuro-muscular system for a more productive response to the final strength-building set.

Interestingly, research with other three-set strength-training programs has not produced such impressive results. For example, the Berger protocol, which requires three sets of six repetitions with the six-repetition maximum (6 RM) weightload elicited only 65% as much strength development as the DeLorme-Watkins protocol (Faigenbaum et al., 1996b). Apparently, three high-effort exercise sets do not represent the most appropriate strength-training protocol for preadolescent boys and girls.

Due primarily to time factors, some youth strength-training studies have incorporated a single set of 10 to 12 different resistance exercises, typically performed on child-sized weight-stack machines (Faigenbaum et al., 1999; 2001; 2002). Although not as productive as the DeLorme-Watkins protocol, single-set programs can be highly effective. Just as importantly, single-set programs are very time efficient, which is a practical consideration for children's fitness programs. For example, youth program participants can begin with about 15 minutes of aerobic warm-up activities, then perform approximately 20 to 30 minutes of strength exercises (one to two sets of eight to 12 exercises) followed by another 15 minutes of aerobic-games activity.

For most practical purposes, children should perform one good set of eight to 12 strength exercises to condition all of their major muscle groups. If time permits, a three-set protocol using progressive warm-up sets may produce even greater strength gains. However, to reduce the risk of overtraining, begin with a range of 10 to 20 total sets in each session. Of course, there are many combinations of sets and exercises to achieve this recommendation.

Speed

Speed of movement has a major influence on the performance of resistance exercise, and on the potential benefits of the strength-training program. Fast lifting speeds require high muscle force to initiate the movement and low muscle force throughout the remainder of the movement. Slow lifting speeds require a relatively even application of muscle force from beginning to end of the exercise movement.

Although various speeds of movement are effective for strength development, slower repetitions are recommended for young exercisers. Movement control and consistent application of force are important training considerations for preadolescents who are learning to perform strength exercise.

One definition of movement control is the ability to stop any lifting or lowering action upon being asked to do so, without momentum carrying the movement to completion. Generally speaking, this level of movement control requires a repetition speed of about three to five seconds. At this speed, a set of 10 repetitions requires 30 to 50 seconds of continuous and controlled muscle activity.

Because muscles are capable of about 40% more force output during lowering movements (eccentric actions) than during lifting movements (concentric actions), children should be instructed to utilize slower speeds on the downward phase of each repetition. This provides a higher strength-building stimulus and a lower risk of injury than fast, gravity-assisted descending actions.

Range

The longer the distance over which force is applied, the more work muscles perform, other factors being equal. Therefore, full-range exercise movements are preferred over abbreviated muscle actions. Of course, exercisers should never move into overstretched or uncomfortable positions, but rather should attain a reasonable range of joint action on every exercise repetition.

Short and choppy movements limit the exercise effectiveness to the range that is trained, which can lead to imbalanced strength development and relative muscle weakness in the joint-flexed and joint-extended positions. Obviously, children benefit most from full-range muscle strength, and should therefore avoid partial movements when performing resistance exercise.

Generally speaking, rotary exercises, such as leg extensions and biceps curls, can be safely performed from joint-flexed to joint-extended positions. However, linear exercises, such as leg presses and chest presses, should not be taken beyond a comfortably stretched position to prevent muscle-tendon strain. For example, the stretched position in the leg-press exercise should not exceed a 90-degree angle at the knee joint, and the backward movement in the chest-press exercise should stop when the hands are even with the chest.

Technique

The key components of proper strength-training exercise technique are speed, range, posture, and execution. As previously discussed, relatively slow movement speed and comfortably full movement range are critical factors for enhancing exercise effectiveness and reducing risk of injury.

Exercise posture refers to a stable and biomechanically correct body position during performance of resistance exercise. Basically, "sitting tall" (head, shoulders, and hips aligned vertically) and "standing tall" (head, shoulders, hips, knees, and ankles aligned vertically) are the most useful cues for eliciting proper posture in young strength exercisers. Because leaning forward, backward, or sideways while lifting weights can place excessive stress on lumbar spine mechanisms, do not permit such reactionary and potentially injurious movements.

Although exercise execution involves every aspect of performing proper repetitions, evenness of movement is of particular concern with young strength-training participants. Any twisting, turning, or otherwise uneven exercise movement should not be permitted in youth strength-training programs. These movements typically result from trying to lift too much weight or attempting to squeeze out an extra repetition without attention to proper technique. Make sure that young people know how to identify these faulty techniques and never resort to these unnecessary and risky actions.

Another aspect of proper execution is the breathing pattern. Teach children to exhale throughout their lifting movements (concentric muscle actions) and to inhale during their lowering movements (eccentric muscle actions). Most importantly, they should never hold their breath when performing strength exercise, as doing so can trigger unnecessary elevations in blood pressure. It is a good idea to have children count their repetitions out-loud, because they cannot hold their breath when doing so.

Progression

Everyone likes to make progress, and youth exercisers seem especially concerned about regularly increasing their training weightloads. Basically, if they do not see at least weekly improvements in strength, children may become discouraged and lose interest in resistance training. To maintain their enthusiasm for this important physical activity, children must see incremental gains in muscle strength. For this reason, as well as for reduced risk of injury from doing too much too soon, use exercise equipment that permits small increases in the training resistance. Generally speaking, a 1- to 2-pound weight increment is preferred for most upper-body exercises, while 3- to 5-pound weight increments typically work well for most leg exercises.

Most strength-training authorities advise increasing the exercise resistance by approximately 5 to 10% at a time (Faigenbaum & Westcott, 2000). For a young boy doing an upper-body exercise with 20 pounds, this requires a 1- to 2-pound increase in the training load. For a young girl performing a leg exercise with 80 pounds, this requires a 4- to 8-pound increment in the training load.

A double progression approach to youth strength training is also recommended. First, using a given weightload, try to increase the number of repetitions performed with proper technique each training session. Second, once a child can complete 15 repetitions with correct form, increase the exercise resistance by approximately 5%. Of course, this will reduce the number of repetitions that can be performed, so the child can now work on increasing the repetitions to 15 before again adding 5% more resistance.

Do not take progression for granted. Consistent increases in both exercise repetitions and weightloads are major motivating factors for young strength-training participants.

Summary

Basic exercise guidelines for safe, sensible, and successful youth strength training are summarized as follows.

Exercise Selection: Perform approximately eight to 12 standard strength exercises that cumulatively address all of the major muscle groups.

Exercise Frequency: Begin with two non-consecutive strength-training sessions per week.

Exercise Resistance: Train with a resistance that is about 60 to 75% of maximum weightload.

Exercise Repetitions: Perform approximately 10 to 15 repetitions of each exercise set.

Exercise Sets: Perform one challenging set of 10 to 15 repetitions for each strength exercise. One or two progressive warm-up or additional sets may be performed if time permits.

Exercise Speed: Use a controlled movement speed, approximately three to five seconds for each repetition.

Exercise Range: Use a full range of joint action for most strength exercises, but avoid moving into positions of discomfort.

Exercise Technique: In addition to controlled movement speed and complete movement range, use proper posture, correct biomechanics, and smooth execution during every exercise set.

Exercise Progression: Increase the exercise resistance by approximately 5 to 10% whenever 15 repetitions can be completed with proper technique.

Strength-training Exercises

CHAPTER FOUR

This chapter presents the basic strength-training exercises that are most appropriate and practical for preadolescent boys and girls. Due to the wide variations in equipment availability, a standard program of youth strength exercises is presented for adult-sized resistance machines, child-sized resistance machines, free-weight equipment, bodyweight resistance, elastic bands, and medicine balls. Regardless of the equipment utilized, train in accordance with the exercise guidelines presented in Chapter Three.

Adult-sized Resistance Machine Exercises

Most youth will fit the linear-action resistance machines found in most fitness centers. Linear-action machines require straight-line movements referred to as pushing or pulling exercises. These include leg presses, chest presses, seated rows, pull-downs, and similar exercises. Unfortunately, smaller youth typically do not fit properly on rotary-action resistance machines designed for adults. Their shorter limbs simply do not align adequately with the machines' axes of rotation. Consequently, adult-sized rotary exercises, such as knee extensions, hamstring curls, triceps extensions, and biceps curls, are not recommended for preadolescents. The following seven exercises provide a relatively comprehensive strength-training program for youth who train on adult-sized resistance machines.

Although this circuit of adult-sized resistance machines exercises addresses most of the major muscle groups, it does not include specific exercises for the trunk muscles.

Therefore, you should add the modified trunk curl (page 54) and birddog trunk extension exercise (page 55) for a more comprehensive, nine-station strength-training workout.

Leg Press

Targeted Muscles: Quadriceps, hamstrings, gluteals

Starting Position: Sit with the full back against the seatback, and with the feet evenly placed on the footpad, the lower legs parallel to the floor, and the knees at a 90-degree angle.

Hold the handgrips, and keep the head up and facing forward (Figure 4.1a).

Exercise Performance: Slowly press the legs forward until the knees are almost straight but not locked-out. Pause and slowly return to the starting position. Exhale during the pressing action and inhale during the return movement (Figure 4.1b).

Figure 4.1a

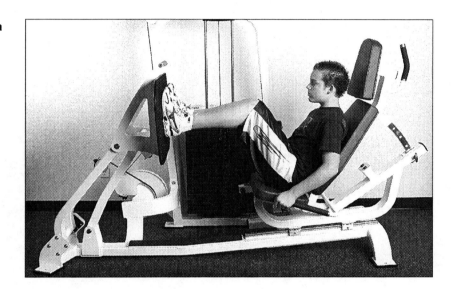

Figure 4.1b

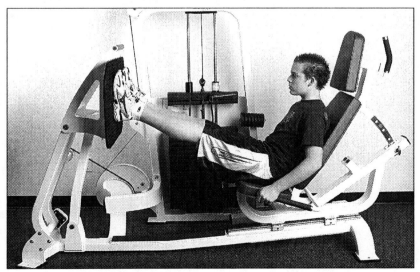

Chest Press

Targeted Muscles: Pectoralis major, anterior deltoid, triceps

Starting Position: Sit with the full back against the seatback, hold the handles at middle-chest level, and keep the head up and facing forward (Figure 4.2a).

Exercise Performance: Slowly press the arms forward until the elbows are extended. Pause and slowly return to the starting position. Exhale during the pressing action and inhale during the return movement (Figure 4.2b).

Figure 4.2a

Figure 4.2b

Seated Row

Targeted Muscles: Latissimus dorsi, teres major, biceps, rhomboids, trapezius, posterior deltoid

Starting Position: In a good sitting posture, hold the handles at middle-chest level, and keep the head up and facing forward (Figure 4.3a).

Exercise Performance: Slowly pull the arms backward until the handles are close to the chest. Pause and slowly return to the starting position. Exhale during the pulling action and inhale during the return movement (Figure 4.3b).

Figure 4.3

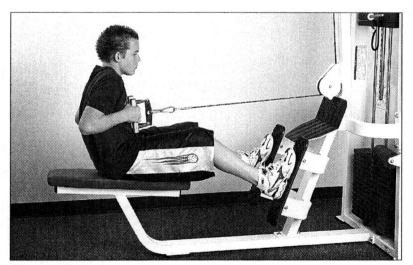

Figure 4.3b

Shoulder Press

Targeted Muscles: Deltoids, triceps, upper trapezius

Starting Position: Sit with the full back against the seatback, hold the handles between chin and shoulder level, and keep the head up and facing forward (Figure 4.4a).

Exercise Performance: Slowly press the arms upward until the elbows are extended. Pause and slowly return to the starting position. Exhale during the pressing action and inhale during the return movement (Figure 4.4b).

Figure 4.4a

Figure 4.4b

Lat Pull-down

Targeted Muscles: Latissimus dorsi, teres major, biceps

Starting Position: With the legs secured beneath the thigh pads, hold the bar with the arms fully extended, and keep the torso erect, and the head up and facing forward (Figure 4.5a).

Exercise Performance: Slowly pull the arms downward until the bar is below chin level. Pause and slowly return to the starting position. Exhale during the pulling action and inhale during the return movement (Figure 4.5b).

Figure 4.5a

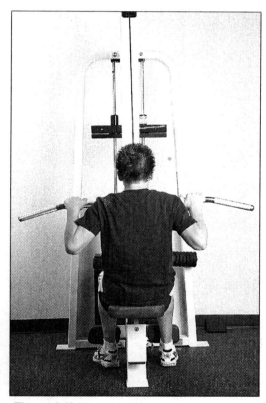

Figure 4.5b

Weight-assisted Bar Dip

Targeted Muscles: Triceps, pectoralis major, anterior deltoid

Starting Position: With knees on the platform and hands on the dip bars with elbows fully extended, keep the torso erect and the head up and facing forward (Figure 4.6a).

Exercise Performance: Slowly lower the body until the elbows are bent at 90 degrees. Pause and slowly the press body upward until the elbows are fully extended. Inhale during the lowering movement and exhale during the upward movement (Figure 4.6b).

Notes: Increasing the weightload on this machine reduces the bodyweight resistance through counterbalance, and thereby reduces intensity. To increase intensity, decrease the weightload on the machine.

Do not allow the shoulders to drop below the elbows on the descent.

Figure 4.6a

Figure 4.6b

Weight-assisted Chin-up

Targeted Muscles: Biceps, latissimus dorsi, teres major

Starting Position: With knees on the platform and hands on the chin bar with elbows extended, hold the torso erect and keep the head up and facing forward (Figure 4.7a).

Exercise Performance: Slowly pull the body upward until the chin is above bar. Inhale during the lowering movement and exhale during the upward movement (Figure 4.7b).

Note: Increasing the weightload on this machine reduces the bodyweight resistance through counterbalance, and thereby reduces intensity. To increase intensity, decrease the weightload on the machine.

Figure 4.7a

Figure 4.7b

Child-sized Resistance Machine Exercises

More and more fitness facilities are providing specially designed resistance equipment for preadolescent boys and girls. Most child-sized resistance machines are similar to adult models on a smaller scale, and are used in essentially the same manner. Other child-sized resistance machines are designed to be more youth friendly, with moving seats that provide a riding action on each exercise. Basically, this type of youth strength-training equipment, which is featured in this section, involves two forms of resistance on every repetition, the external weightstack resistance and the internal bodyweight resistance.

Add the modified trunk curl (page 54) and birddog trunk extension exercise (page 55) to the seven linear-action weightstack machine exercises to provide a relatively comprehensive nine-station strength-training program.

Leg Press

Targeted Muscles: Quadriceps, hamstrings, gluteals

Starting Position: Sit with the full back against the seatback, with the feet evenly placed on the footpads, the lower legs approximately parallel to the floor, and the knees bent at an almost 90-degree angle. Hold the handgrips, and keep the head up and facing forward (Figure 4.8a).

Exercise Performance: Slowly extend the legs until the knees are almost straight, but not locked-out. Pause and slowly return to the starting position. Exhale during the pushing action and inhale during the return movement (Figure 4.8b).

Note: The seat will move backward and upward during the pushing action.

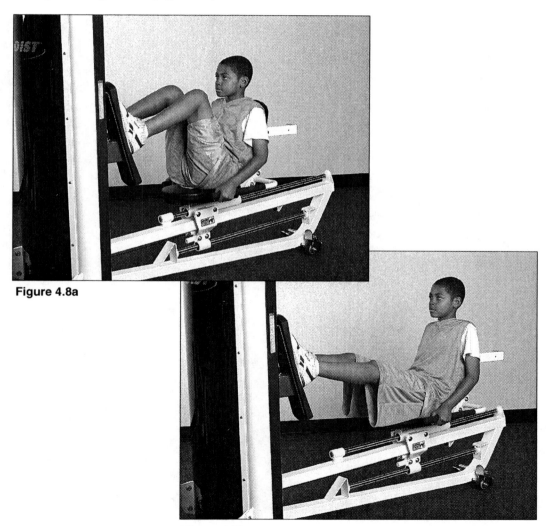

Figure 4.8a

Figure 4.8b

Squat Press

Targeted Muscles: Quadriceps, hamstrings, gluteals

Starting Position: Sit with the full back against the seatback, with the feet evenly placed on the footpads, the lower legs approximately parallel to the floor, and the knees bent at an almost 90-degree angle. Hold the handgrips, and keep the head up and facing forward (Figure 4.9a).

Exercise Performance: Slowly extend the legs until the knees are almost straight, but not locked-out. Pause and slowly return to the starting position. Exhale during the pushing action and inhale during the return movement (Figure 4.9b).

Note: The seat will move backward and upward during the pushing action.

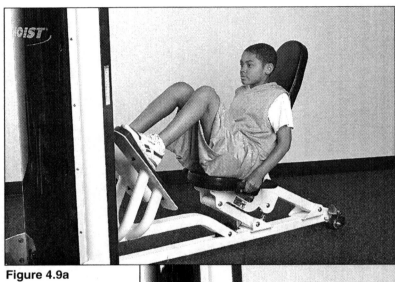

Figure 4.9a

Figure 4.9b

Bench Press

Targeted Muscles: Pectoralis major, anterior deltoid, triceps

Starting Position: Sit with the full back against the seatback, with the feet evenly placed on the footpads, and the knees bent at a 90-degree angle. Hold the handgrips, and keep the head up and facing forward (Figure 4.10a).

Exercise Performance: Slowly extend the arms until the elbows are straight but not locked out. Pause and slowly return to the starting position. Exhale during the pushing action and inhale during the return movement (Figure 4.10b).

Note: The seat will move backward and upward during the pushing action.

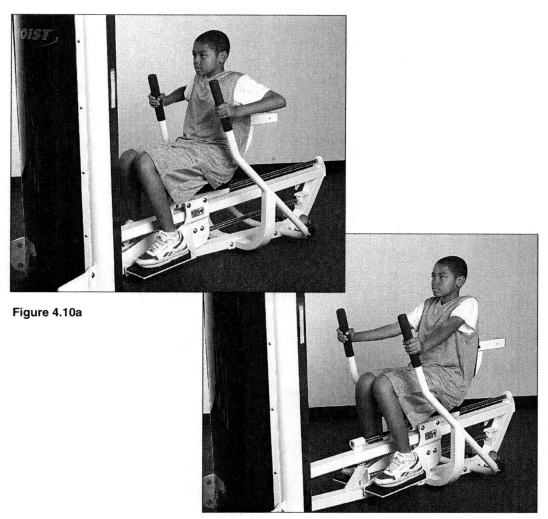

Figure 4.10a

Figure 4.10b

Mid Row

Targeted Muscles: Latissimus dorsi, teres major, biceps, rhomboids, trapezius, posterior deltoid

Starting Position: Sit with the chest against the seat pad and the feet on the foot rests. Hold the handles at mid-chest level, and keep the head up and facing forward (Figure 4.11a).

Exercise Performance: Slowly pull the elbows backward until the chest is close to the handles. Pause and slowly return to the starting position. Exhale during the pulling action and inhale during the return movement (Figure 4.11b).

Note: The seat will move forward and upward during the pulling action.

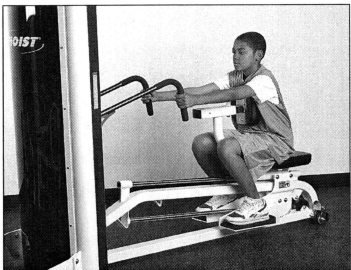

Figure 4.11a

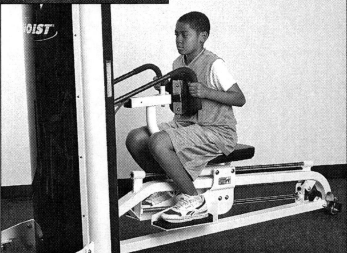

Figure 4.11b

Shoulder Press

Targeted Muscles: Deltoids, triceps, upper trapezius

Starting Position: Sit with the full back against the seatback and the feet on the foot rests. Hold the handles between chin and shoulder level, and keep the head up and facing forward (Figure 4.12a).

Exercise Performance: Slowly extend the arms until the elbows are straight. Pause and slowly return to the starting position. Exhale during the pushing action and inhale during the return movement (Figure 4.12b).

Note: The seat will move backward and upward during the pushing action.

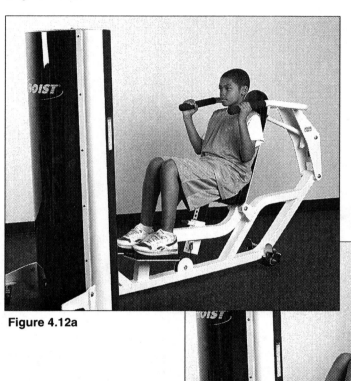

Figure 4.12a

Figure 4.12b

Chin-up

Targeted Muscles: Biceps, latissimus dorsi, teres major

Starting Position: Sit with the legs secured beneath the thigh pads and feet on the foot rests. Hold the bar with an underhand grip with arms fully extended, and keep the torso erect with the head up and facing forward (Figure 4.13a).

Exercise Performance: Slowly pull the arms downward until the chin is above the bar. Pause and slowly return to the starting position. Exhale during the pulling action and inhale during the return movement (Figure 4.13b).

Note: The seat will move upward and forward during the pulling action.

Figure 4.13a

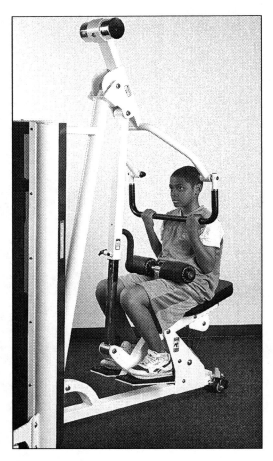

Figure 4.13b

Seated Dip

Targeted Muscles: Triceps, pectoralis major, anterior deltoid

Starting Position: Sit with the full back against the seatback, and the feet on the foot rests. Hold the handles below the shoulders, and keep the head in line with the torso (Figure 4.14a).

Exercise Performance: Slowly extend the arms until the elbows are straight. Pause and slowly return to the starting position. Exhale during the pushing action and inhale during the return movement (Figure 4.14b).

Notes: The seat will move backward and upward during the pushing action.

Do not allow the shoulders to drop below the elbows on the descent.

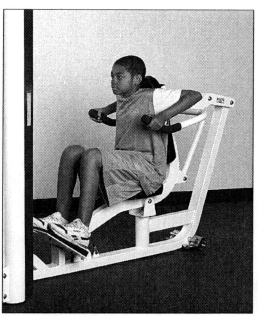

Figure 4.14a

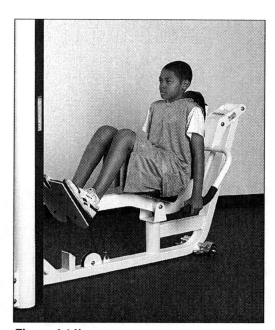

Figure 4.14b

Free-weight Equipment Exercises

If resistance machines are unavailable, children can train safely and effectively with free-weight equipment. Although barbells may be used for many exercises, barbell squats and barbell bench presses must be carefully spotted by a competent adult instructor due to the inherent danger of being trapped beneath the weight on a failed repetition. For this reason, dumbbells are preferable for youth strength-training programs that use free-weight equipment. The following seven dumbbell exercises address all of the major muscle groups when combined with modified trunk curls (page 54) and birddog trunk extensions (page 55) for a nine-station strength-training workout.

Dumbbell Squats

Targeted Muscles: Quadriceps, hamstrings, gluteals

Starting Position: Stand tall, with a dumbbell in each hand and arms extended. Keep the feet shoulder-width apart, and the head up and facing forward (Figure 4.15a).

Exercise Performance: Slowly move the hips downward and backward until the knees are bent 90 degrees. Pause and slowly raise the hips to the starting position. Inhale during the downward movement and exhale during the upward movement. Keep the torso as erect as possible throughout each repetition (Figure 4.15b).

Note: Some youth may not be able to perform a full squat. Have them progress from a limited-depth squat until they are able to move through the full range of motion.

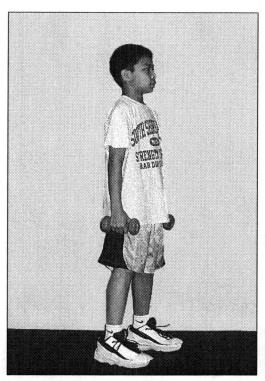

Figure 4.15a

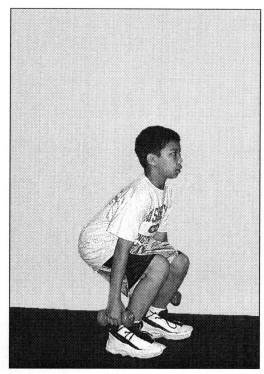

Figure 4.15b

Dumbbell Bench Press

Targeted Muscles: Pectoralis major, anterior deltoid, triceps

Starting Position: Keep the head, back, and hips on a bench with the feet flat on the floor. Hold the dumbbells with the arms extended above the chest (Figure 4.16a).

Exercise Performance: Slowly move the arms downward and outward until the dumbbells are near the sides of the chest. Pause and slowly press the dumbbells up to the starting position. Inhale during the downward movement and exhale during the upward movement. Keep the hips on the bench and the dumbbells level on every repetition (Figure 4.16b).

Figure 4.16a

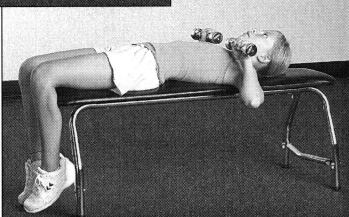

Figure 4.16b

Dumbbell Bent Row

Targeted Muscles: Latissimus dorsi, teres major, biceps, rhomboids, trapezius, posterior deltoid

Starting Position: With the left foot on the floor, the right knee on the bench, and the right hand on the bench, hold a dumbbell in the left hand with the arm extended downward. Keep the back parallel to the floor, and the head up and facing downward (Figure 4.17a).

Exercise Performance: Slowly pull the left arm upward until the dumbbell lightly touches the chest. Pause and slowly lower the dumbbell to the starting position. Exhale during the upward movement and inhale during the downward movement (Figure 4.17b). After completing the exercise set, reverse hand and leg positions and perform a second set using the right arm.

Figure 4.17a

Figure 4.17b

Dumbbell Shoulder Press

Targeted Muscles: Deltoids, triceps, upper trapezius

Starting Position: Stand tall, holding the dumbbells just above the shoulders. Keep the feet shoulder-width apart, and the head up and facing forward (Figure 4.18a).

Exercise Performance: Slowly press the arms upward until the elbows are extended and dumbbells are overhead. Pause and slowly lower the dumbbells to the starting position. Exhale during the upward movement and inhale during the lowering movement. Keep the torso straight throughout each exercise repetition (Figure 4.18b).

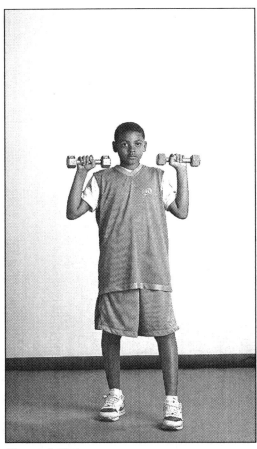

Figure 4.18a

Figure 4.18b

Dumbbell Biceps Curl

Targeted Muscles: Biceps

Starting Position: Stand tall, holding the dumbbells with the arms extended downward. Keep the feet shoulder-width apart, and the head up and facing forward (Figure 4.19a).

Exercise Performance: Slowly curl the dumbbells upward until the elbows are fully flexed. Pause and slowly lower the dumbbells to the starting position. Exhale during the upward movement and inhale during the downward movement and keep the elbows directly above the hips throughout each repetition (Figure 4.19b).

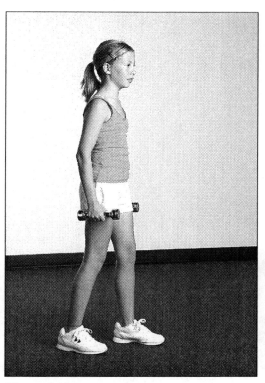

Figure 4.19a

Figure 4.19b

Dumbbell Triceps Extension

Targeted Muscles: Triceps

Starting Position: Stand tall, holding the dumbbell with both hands with the arms extended overhead. Slowly lower the dumbbell behind the head until the elbows are bent 90 degrees. Keep the feet shoulder-width apart, and the head up and facing forward (Figure 4.20a).

Exercise Performance: Slowly extend the elbows upward. Inhale during the downward movement and exhale during the upward movement. Keep the torso straight throughout each exercise repetition (Figure 4.20b).

Figure 4.20a

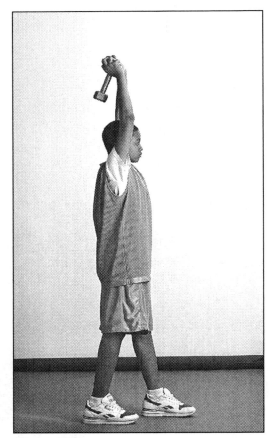

Figure 4.20b

Dumbbell Calf Raise

Targeted Muscles: Gastrocnemius, soleus

Starting Position: Stand tall on a step, holding the dumbbells with the arms extended, and the feet less than shoulder-width apart. Keep the head up and facing forward (Figure 4.21a).

Exercise Performance: Slowly rise onto the toes of both feet and lift the heels as high as possible. Pause and slowly lower to the starting position. Exhale during the upward movement and inhale during the downward movement. Keep torso straight throughout each exercise repetition (Figure 4.21b).

Note: If a child struggles with their balance during this movement, have him or her hold only one dumbbell, and then place the step next to a wall so the free hand can touch the wall for balance.

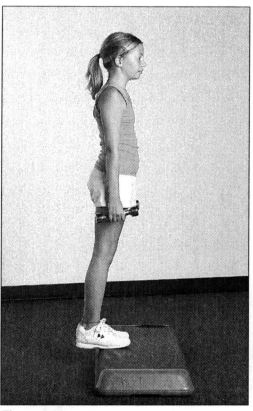

Figure 4.21a

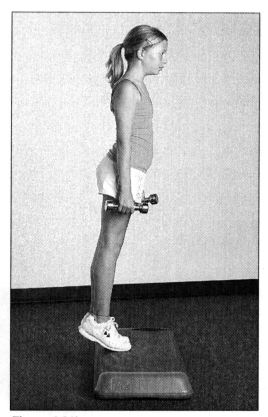

Figure 4.21b

Bodyweight Exercises

I f external resistance exercises, such as those using adult-sized machines, child-sized machines, free-weight equipment, elastic bands, or medicine balls are not an option, have youngsters perform several strength-building exercises using bodyweight resistance. Because bodyweight exercises do not permit progressive increases in resistance, the most common way to accommodate gains in muscle strength and endurance is to add repetitions. This works well up to approximately 20 repetitions, at which point the resistance is too low to promote optimal strength development. Generally speaking, bodyweight exercises are safe and productive when five to 20 repetitions can be performed with correct technique. Pay particular attention to proper posture when performing bodyweight exercises.

Squat

Targeted Muscles: Quadriceps, hamstrings, gluteals

Starting Position: Stand tall with arms extended forward and feet shoulder-width apart. Keep the head up and facing forward (Figure 4.22a).

Exercise Performance: Slowly move the hips downward and backward until the knees are bent 90 degrees. Pause, and slowly raise the hips to the starting position. Inhale during the downward movement and exhale during the upward movement, and keep the torso as erect as possible throughout each repetition (Figure 4.22b).

Note: Some youth may not be able to perform a full squat. Have them progress from a limited-depth squat until they are able to move through the full range of motion.

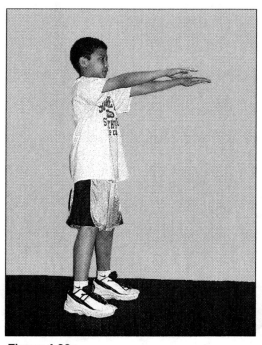

Figure 4.22a

Figure 4.22b

Modified Trunk Curl

Targeted Muscle: Rectus abdominis

Starting Position: In a supine position, place the hands behind the head or cross the arms across the chest and flex one knee as shown (Figure 4.23a).

Exercise Performance: Raise the head and shoulders off the floor while maintaining a neutral spine, pause, and then return to the starting position (Figure 4.23b). Alternate the bent leg midway through each set of repetitions.

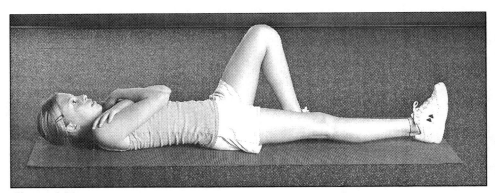

Figure 4.23a

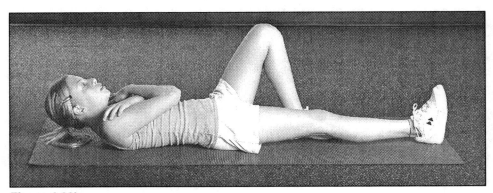

Figure 4.23b

Birddog Trunk Extension

Targeted Muscles: Lumbar extensors (longissimus, iliocostalis, mutifidi)

Starting Position: Begin in an all-fours position.

Exercise Performance: Extend one leg and the opposite arm so that they are parallel to the floor (Figure 4.24). Hold this position for seven to eight seconds, and then repeat with the opposite arm and leg.

Figure 4.24

Push-up

Targeted Muscles: Pectoralis major, anterior deltoid, triceps, rectus abdominis

Starting Position: Begin in a prone plank position, with toes on the floor, legs straight, hands beneath the shoulders, and fingers pointing forward. Keep the arms extended, the body straight, and the head in line with the torso (Figure 4.25a).

Exercise Performance: Slowly lower the body until the chest nearly contacts the floor. Pause and slowly push the body up to the starting position. Inhale during the lowering movement and exhale during the pushing action (Figure 4.25b).

Note: Keep the body straight throughout every repetition. If standard push-ups are too challenging, place the knees on the floor to reduce bodyweight resistance.

Figure 4.25a

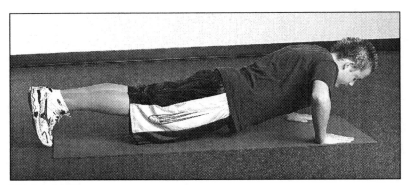

Figure 4.25b

Chair Dip

Targeted Muscles: Pectoralis major, anterior deltoid, triceps

Starting Position: With the hands on the front edge of a chair or bench, extend the arms and keep the heels on the floor with the legs straight. Keep the hips in front of the chair seat, and the head up and facing forward (Figure 4.26a).

Exercise Performance: Slowly lower the body toward the floor until the elbows are bent at a 90-degree angle. Pause and press the body up to the starting position. Inhale during the lowering movement and exhale during the pushing action (Figure 4.26b).

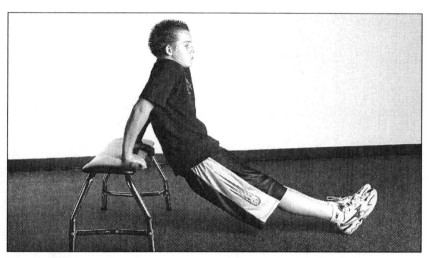

Figure 4.26a

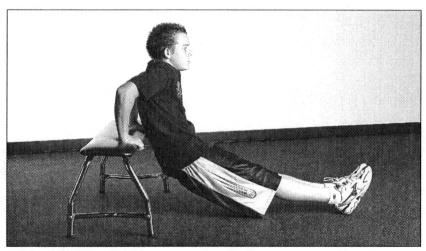

Figure 4.26b

Chin-up

Targeted Muscles: Biceps, latissimus dorsi, teres major, rectus abdominis

Starting Position: With hands on the bar with an underhand grip and arms fully extended, keep the body straight and the head up and facing forward (Figure 4.27a).

Exercise Performance: Slowly pull the body upward until the chin is above the bar. Pause and slowly return to the starting position. Exhale during the pulling action and inhale during the lowering movement (Figure 4.27b).

Note: It may be necessary for an instructor to manually assist the student in the upward phase of the chin-up.

Figure 4.27a

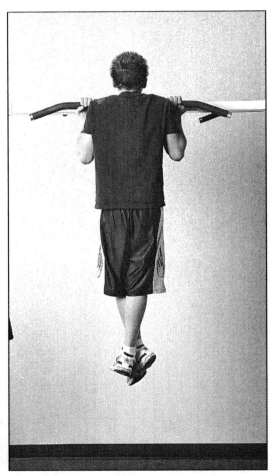

Figure 4.27b

Elastic Band Exercises

Elastic bands are an inexpensive and effective alternative to weight machines and free weights. They are available in different lengths and sizes so each child can start at a safe level and gradually progress. Instructors can adjust the amount of resistance by changing a child's hand position or distance from a fixed object. In some cases, children may need to grasp a section of the elastic band rather than the handles to begin the exercise with an appropriate amount of resistance. As strength improves, resistance can be increased by adjusting the amount of stretch on the band or by using a thicker cord.

Although a spotter is not normally needed for elastic-band training, remind children to maintain proper exercise technique and firmly grasp the elastic band with both hands. This is particularly important at the end of each repetition because resistance from elastic bands is greatest when the exercise motion nears completion. Provide clear instructions and remind children that they can get hurt if they do not use equipment properly.

Elastic Band Squat

Targeted Muscles: Quadriceps, hamstrings, gluteals

Starting Position: Stand tall with both feet on the middle of the band and the hands at shoulder level, palms forward (Figure 4.28a).

Exercise Performance: Slowly lower the hips until the thighs are parallel to the floor, while keeping the back flat and head up. Pause, then return to the starting position by straightening the knees and hips (Figure 4.28b).

Note: Some youth may not be able to perform a full squat. Have them progress from a limited-depth squat until they are able to move through the full range of motion.

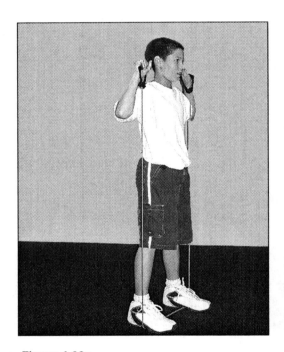

Figure 4.28a

Figure 4.28b

Elastic Band Chest Press

Targeted Muscles: Pectoralis major, anterior deltoid, triceps

Starting Position: Stand tall with feet about shoulder-width apart. Wrap the elastic band around the back and position both hands in front of the shoulders (Figure 4.29a).

Exercise Performance: Straighten the elbows until both arms are extended. Pause, and then return to the starting position (Figure 4.29b).

Note: You may have to tie off some of the elastic band to create the appropriate resistance.

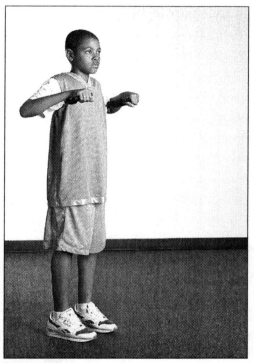

Figure 4.29a

Figure 4.29b

Elastic Band Seated Row

Targeted Muscles: Latissimus dorsi, biceps

Starting Position: Sit on the floor and wrap the elastic band around both feet. Grasp both handles with arms extended and knees slightly bent (Figure 4.30a).

Exercise Performance: Pull the handles back to the sides of the body while keeping the back straight. Pause, and then slowly return to the starting position (Figure 4.30b).

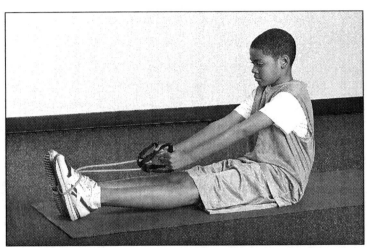

Figure 4.30a

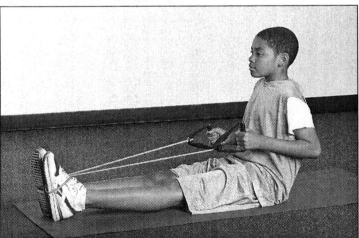

Figure 4.30b

Elastic Band Seated Shoulder Press

Targeted Muscles: Deltoid, upper trapezius, triceps

Starting Position: Sit on the middle of an elastic band and hold the ends of the band at shoulder level, palms forward (Figure 4.31a).

Exercise Performance: Push both arms upward while keeping the back straight. Pause, and then lower arms to the starting position (Figure 4.31b).

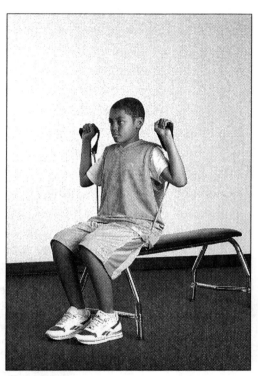

Figure 4.31a

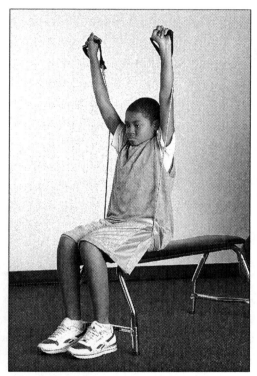

Figure 4.31b

Elastic Band Upright Row

Targeted Muscles: Deltoid, upper trapezius, biceps

Starting Position: Stand with both feet on top of the middle of a band. Hold the band so it hangs straight down in front of the body. Keep the hands facing the body (Figure 4.32a).

Exercise Performance: Pull both hands up to upper-chest level while keeping the elbows slightly higher than the shoulders. Pause, and then lower to the starting position (Figure 4.32b).

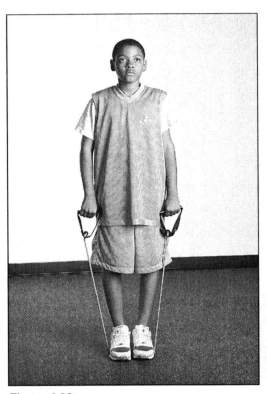

Figure 4.32a

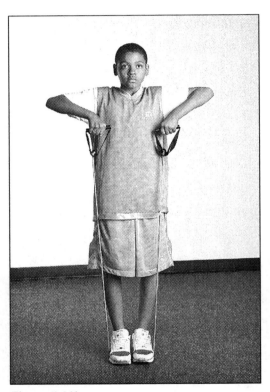

Figure 4.32b

Elastic Band Lateral Raise

Targeted Muscles: Deltoid

Starting Position: Stand with both feet on top of the middle of a band. Hold the band so it hangs straight down along the sides of the body. Keep the palms facing the body (Figure 4.33a).

Exercise Performance: Lift both arms up and to the sides until the arms are level with the shoulders. Pause, and then lower to the starting position. Keep the elbows slightly bent and the back straight throughout the exercise (Figure 4.33b).

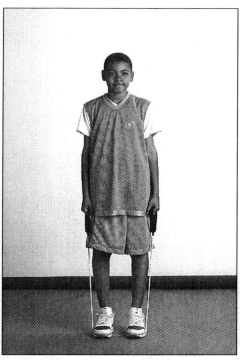

Figure 4.33a

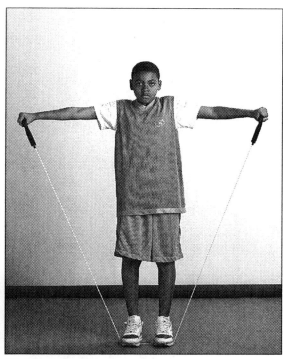

Figure 4.33b

Elastic Band Biceps Curl

Targeted Muscles: Biceps

Starting Position: Stand with both feet on top of the middle of a band. Hold the band so it hangs straight down along the sides of the body. Keep the palms facing forward (Figure 4.34a).

Exercise Performance: Curl both hands upward to the shoulders until the palms face the chest. Pause, and then lower both arms to the starting position (Figure 4.34b).

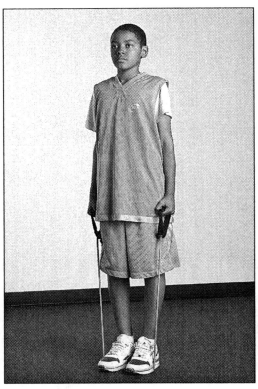

Figure 4.34a

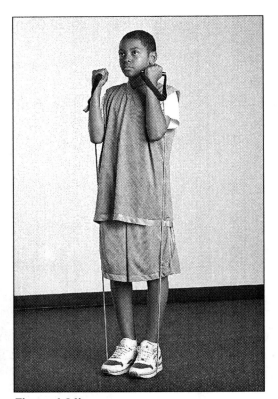

Figure 4.34b

Medicine Ball Exercises

Medicine balls are weighted balls that come in a variety of sizes and colors. They can add a new dimension to a child's strength-training program because they condition the body through dynamic movements that can be performed either slowly or rapidly. While medicine balls are typically used to perform traditional squatting and pressing exercises, you can create your own exercises with medicine balls that involve throwing, catching, and rotating movements. Not only can medicine balls be used to strengthen the upper and lower body, but they also can be particularly effective for strengthening the abdominals, hips, and lower-back musculature.

The intensity of medicine-ball exercises is controlled by varying the weight of the ball and, when appropriate, the distance between training partners. Begin with 1-kilogram balls (about the size of a volleyball) and focus on developing proper exercise technique. As always, remind children that it is important to maintain proper exercise technique throughout the full range of motion. Use color-coded balls so both instructors and participants can easily keep track of the loads they are using.

Medicine Ball Squat

Targeted Muscles: Quadriceps, hamstrings, gluteals

Starting Position: Stand tall holding a medicine ball close to the chest and keep the feet about hip-width apart (Figure 4.35a).

Exercise Performance: Lower the hips until the thighs are parallel to the floor while keeping the back flat and the head up. Pause, and then return to the starting position by straightening the knees and hips (Figure 4.35b).

Note: Some youth may not be able to perform a full squat. Have them progress from a limited-depth squat until they are able to move through the full range of motion.

Figure 4.35a

Figure 4.35b

Medicine Ball Lunge

Targeted Muscles: Quadriceps, hamstrings, gluteals

Starting Position: Stand tall holding a medicine ball close to the chest and the feet about hip-width apart (Figure 4.36a).

Exercise Performance: Take a long step forward while keeping the upper torso erect. Lunge forward far enough so the front knee is bent nearly 90 degrees. Pause, and then return to the starting position and repeat on the other side (Figure 4.36b).

Note: To increase the difficulty of this exercise, move the medicine ball to the right and left during the exercise.

Figure 4.36a

Figure 4.36b

Medicine Ball Push

Targeted Muscles: Pectoralis major, anterior deltoid, triceps

Starting Position: Stand tall holding a medicine ball close to the chest and feet about shoulder-width apart (Figure 4.37a).

Exercise Performance: Quickly press the ball toward the floor and then catch it as it bounces back to the starting position (Figure 4.37b).

Note: The exercise can also be performed with a partner by bounce-passing the ball back and forth.

Figure 4.37a

Figure 4.37b

Medicine Ball Pullover

Targeted Muscles: Latissimus dorsi, serratus anterior, biceps

Starting Position: Stand tall holding a medicine ball behind the head with the elbows slightly bent and feet about shoulder-width apart (Figure 4.38a).

Exercise Performance: Quickly pull the ball overhead and heave the ball toward the floor. Catch the ball as it bounces back to the starting position (Figure 4.38b).

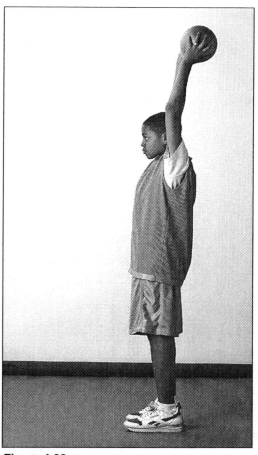

Figure 4.38a

Figure 4.38b

Medicine Ball Triceps Extension

Targeted Muscles: Triceps

Starting Position: Stand tall holding a medicine ball behind the head with elbows bent at ear level (Figure 4.39a).

Exercise Performance: Press the ball overhead until arms are fully extended. Pause, and then return to the starting position (Figure 4.39b).

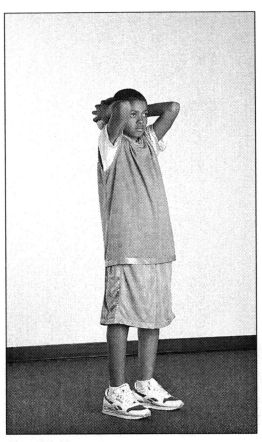

Figure 4.39a

Figure 4.39b

Medicine Ball Abdominal Curl

Targeted Muscles: Rectus abdominis

Starting Position: Lie face-up on the floor holding a medicine ball in front of the body with knees bent (Figure 4.40a).

Exercise Performance: Slowly curl the upper back off the floor while keeping the lower back against the floor. Pause when the abdominal muscles are fully contracted, and then slowly return to the starting position (Figure 4.40b).

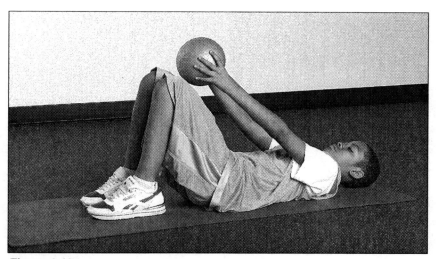

Figure 4.40a

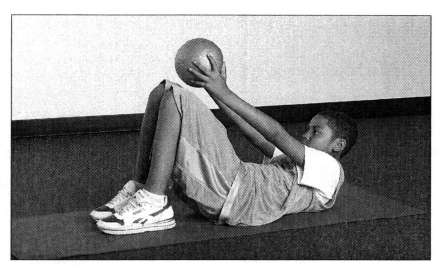

Figure 4.40b

Medicine Ball Partner Twist

Targeted Muscles: Rectus abdominis, external obliques

Starting Position: Stand back to back about 1 foot from a partner with hips forward and knees slightly bent. Hold a medicine ball at waist level (Figure 4.41a).

Exercise Performance: Pass the ball to each other by twisting the torso. Complete the desired number of repetitions, and then change direction (Figure 4.41b).

Figure 4.41a

Figure 4.41b

Medicine Ball Up and Over

Targeted Muscles: Deltoids, rectus abdominis, erector spinae, quadriceps, gluteals, hamstrings

Starting Position: Stand back to back about 1 to 2 feet from a partner. Hold a medicine ball at waist level (Figure 4.42a).

Exercise Performance: Pass the ball overhead, and then squat slightly to retrieve the ball between the knees (Figure 4.42b). Complete the desired number of repetitions, and then change direction.

Figure 4.42a

Figure 4.42b

Summary

Instructors can use different modes of strength training to enhance the muscular fitness of children. In addition to weight machines, free weights, and bodyweight exercises, elastic bands and medicine balls can be used to add variety to a child's strength-training program. Give every child an opportunity to learn about different training methods and gradually add new exercises to their exercise programs. While each mode of training has its advantages and disadvantages, the key is to provide clear instructions and begin each exercise with an appropriate amount of resistance.

Teaching Tools

and Program

Design

Most of us have received instruction in sports skills during physical education programs or group exercise classes. However, fewer individuals have had much formal education in the area of strength training. The typical introduction to resistance exercise is a one-time demonstration, during which the instructor shows you how to perform a circuit of weightstack machines and gives you a workout log to record your training progress. This brief orientation is less than optimal for adults, and such an approach is definitely inadequate for children.

CHAPTER FIVE

Safe and successful youth strength-training programs require a strong teaching emphasis with careful instruction, close supervision, and appropriate program design. Here are some of the teaching tools and program-design components that you can incorporate into youth strength-training programs.

Attitude

Effective teaching is as much about motivation as it is about education, and this is particularly true for working with children. Teacher attitude sets the tone for learning and performing the essential skills with enthusiasm, as well as for giving sufficient physical effort to experience training results. Attitude is everything as far as young people are concerned. Children prefer teachers who are encouraging and supportive, and have a caring attitude toward each student's personal progress.

You can project a positive attitude by welcoming each child to class, calling everyone by name, encouraging exercise efforts, reinforcing physical performance, and thanking each child for participating in the exercise session. Young people tend to model their instructor's behavior, and a positive teacher attitude may be the best means for eliciting positive student attitudes in a strength-training setting (Westcott, 1980).

Atmosphere

An inviting exercise facility is clean, well-lit, well-ventilated, well-organized, neatly arranged, and uncluttered. Although the atmosphere in the strength-training facility should not feel like a library, neither should it resemble a free-for-all playground environment. Due to the inherent potential for injury, the weight-room atmosphere should be one of controlled activity with a high level of structure and supervision, a few key behavioral rules, and some basic exercise guidelines for training sensibly and safely. Of course, an appropriate exercise atmosphere is one of acceptance for all youth participants and approval for all levels of achievement.

Performance Feedback

Everyone likes to get feedback when they are doing well. Appropriate performance feedback provides reinforcement for what an exerciser is doing right and recommendations for what he or she could do better, which is called corrective feedback. In a sense, it is similar to seeing a video of one's self in action through the eyes of a competent instructor.

Obviously, you must fully understand the task, carefully observe the performance, and clearly communicate pertinent feedback information to the exerciser. Generally speaking, give at least two positive feedback statements for each corrective feedback statement. This encourages the participant by emphasizing what has been mastered over what has yet to be learned.

From a psychological perspective, performance feedback assures the exerciser that you are actively involved in the teaching-learning process, and really want the student to succeed. Moderate amounts of performance feedback may be more productive than overwhelming amounts of technical infor-mation (Westcott et al., 2003). Therefore, it is important to provide clear and concise feedback statements on those aspects of the exercise performance that are most important for successful program participation.

Positive Reinforcement

Positive reinforcement is a highly effective means of motivating desired behaviors in young people. However, it must be seen as both deserved and sincere for best results. Simply saying "good job" or "you're looking good" has little meaningful impact on young people's performance. Instead, positive feedback is most beneficial when it is coupled with relevant performance feedback. For example, a comment such as, "Good job, John. You exhaled during the lifting movement and inhaled during the lowering movement," indicates that you carefully observed the exercise efforts and are

pleased with specific aspects of John's physical performance. John now knows that he did certain things correctly and that his instructor was satisfied. Of course, this makes it more likely that he will repeat these desirable training actions and make better progress as a result.

Positive reinforcement may be given nonverbally as well, via a big smile, a pat on the back, a handshake, a high-five, a hand-clap, or two thumbs up. Children respond just as favorably to nonverbal positive reinforcement, as long as it is sincere and deserved.

Although positive reinforcement may have the most impact during or immediately after exercise performance, it is also useful at the end of the training session. Checking the students' workout cards just before they leave and praising their personal progress reinforces participation and increases the likelihood of enthusiastic return to the next exercise session.

Communication Skills

A large-scale survey conducted across the East Coast of the United States revealed the most important charac-teristics that thousands of exercise participants looked for in ideal fitness instructors. Second only to "knowledge of physical fitness" was "communication (teaching) skills" (Westcott, 1991). Basically, exercisers want instructors who, first, have an excellent understanding of exercise science, and second, have the ability to clearly communicate that knowledge to others. Good communication skills are essential for safe and successful youth strength-training programs, including precise demonstrations and concise explanations. Simple statements, singleness of purpose, and clear focus on the main task are all parts of good communication. Question-and-answer techniques are highly effective with children, and you should always encourage two-way communication during the exercise session. Using first names and making eye contact tend to enhance communication efforts with young people by making conversations more personal and respectful.

The key to teaching new exercises and training procedures to youth is to address one task at a time. That is, focus on one aspect of the exercise performance until it is mastered, then address another aspect with singular focus in a progressive sequence of simple learning steps that makes sense to the students. Having good communication skills with youth is about being clear and concise, basic and brief.

Introductory Sessions

Perhaps the most important period of any youth strength-training program is the introductory sessions. It is during this time that the children quickly develop either approach tendencies or avoidance tendencies toward resistance exercise. A large part of a child's response to the activity is related to how much attention he or she receives, how much success is perceived and how much enjoyment is experienced in the class environment. Quite simply, if an elective physical activity is not fun, most children will soon find a different way to spend their free time.

Because first impressions have a major influence on young people, it is imperative for all of the strength-training staff to be highly encouraging and enthusiastic, especially during the introductory sessions. Quickly convey that the activity is important and that each child is important. You must also convince the participants that the benefits of strength training are really meaningful and important.

Fortunately, due to the neurological (motor learning) component of muscular conditioning, new exercisers should see strength improvement with each workout as they perform the repetitions with progressively heavier weightloads during the initial training sessions. Of course, the reinforcement aspect of using more resistance must be balanced with the safety aspects of proper exercise form and gradual training progressions.

Attentive instruction and supervision cannot be overemphasized during the introductory sessions, so that each boy and girl feels like a valued participant in the training program. High levels of instructor attention are also necessary during the initial exercise sessions to assess each child's physiological and psychological characteristics, and to adjust the teaching format accordingly. For example, participants may have varying levels of energy and independence, and some will be more talkative than others. Attending to each individual in the most appropriate manner is a major motivating factor during the initial exercise sessions, and throughout the training program.

Warm-up

The warm-up period serves several purposes, including physiological preparation for the subsequent strength-training exercises. After a period of low-to-moderate intensity aerobic activity, a warmed up musculoskeletal system should be more responsive to high-effort resistance exercise and less prone to injury.

Another goal of the warm-up period is to burn additional calories through intermittent large-muscle activities and to provide some degree of cardiovascular conditioning. Dynamic stretching can be easily incorporated into the warm-up activities, thereby enhancing the children's joint flexibility. In addition to the performance of traditional static stretching exercises, dynamic stretching involves the performance of low-, moderate-, and high-intensity movements that are designed to elevate core body temperature, enhance motor unit excitability, improve kinesthetic awareness, and maximize active ranges of motion. This type of warm-up protocol typically includes hops, skips, jumps, and various movement-based exercises for the upper and lower body. Warm-up protocols that include dynamic stretching have been shown to positively influence muscle function in adults (Gullich & Schmidtbleicher, 1996; Young & Behm, 2003), and it is likely that similar consequences would be observed in youth.

Non-competitive games involving various balls and hand-held implements can be useful for improving a variety of motor abilities, including throwing, catching, kicking, and striking skills. Creative use of cones, wands, hoops, and other apparatus can help students develop better locomotor skills, including running, jumping, skipping, and hopping. For more information about non-competitive group activities, see ACE's *Youth Fitness* book.

Warm-up periods permit group activity in which classmates work together to achieve specific goals in an enjoyable and non-threatening manner. Teamwork and talk, huffing and puffing, getting the kinks out, and recharging the activity batteries are all important aspects of the warm-up period. Generally speaking, the warm-up should be an exciting and enjoyable segment of the exercise session. Simple games, group relays, follow the leader, and a variety of other movement activities can be included in an effective warm-up period.

Cool-Down

The cool-down period is essentially the same as the warm-up period, but with a reverse progression of exercise intensity. The primary purpose of the warm-up period is to transition from a resting state to a physically active state, whereas the primary purpose of the cool-down is to transition from a physically active state to a resting state. The activities that work well for the warm-up session work equally well for the cool-down session.

The majority of the cool-down period should be large-muscle, aerobic activity at a moderate intensity in a game-like atmosphere. However, during the final minutes of the cool-down period incorporate lower-intensity activities, including stretches and relaxation exercises. In some ways, the cool-down activities represent a reward for completing the strength-training session, and the children should have fun during this period of the exercise class.

In a typical one-hour class session, allot about five minutes for checking in, daily instructions, and introductory dialogue, 15 minutes for the warm-up activities, 20 to 30 minutes for the strength exercises, and 15 minutes for the cool-down activities.

Educational Emphasis

Throughout each exercise class, and especially during the introductory dialogue, provide pertinent learning experiences with essential educational information related to health, fitness, and nutrition. Emphasize strength-training principles and procedures, while also addressing aerobic conditioning, stretching exercises, locomotor patterns, basic sports skills, and sensible nutrition.

In addition to sharing relevant information in a formal manner, provide as many educational experiences as possible during each exercise session. This includes taking advantage of teachable moments, as well as training the participants to record their own workout cards, make appropriate increases in their exercise weightloads, analyze their own exercise technique, and encourage their classmates as they perform the exercises.

Discuss the strength exercises in terms of the major muscles they address, so the children learn, for example, where the quadriceps are located and what movements they produce. Also, relate how stronger quadriceps should help them to perform better in activities that emphasize these muscles, such as jumping, sprinting, and kicking.

Of course, part of the educational process is to teach enough about the "why" and "how" of sensible strength training so that children can share this information with friends and classmates. By doing so, they may encourage their peers to also join a supervised program of strength exercise and benefit accordingly. An appropriate educational emphasis enables youth to perform strength exercise with greater competence and confidence, which in turn enhances their training commitment.

Summary

To lead effective and enjoyable youth strength-training sessions, you must use successful teaching strategies and appropriate program design. Among the essential teaching tools are: (1) positive instructor attitudes; (2) a class atmosphere characterized by acceptance and approval; (3) clear and concise feedback on the most important aspects of exercise performance; (4) relevant positive reinforcement that is perceived as both sincere and deserved; (5) good communication skills that feature simple statements, singleness of purpose, and clear focus; (6) enthusiastic introductory sessions that include attentive instruction and supervision; (7) energetic warm-up periods; (8) enjoyable cool-down periods; and (9) pervasive educational emphasis that produces competent and confident youth strength-training participants. Properly applied, these teaching tools should enhance children's strength-training experiences and encourage continued exercise participation.

Designing Youth Strength-training Sessions

Youth instructors have a unique opportunity to promote physical activity and enhance the long-term health and well-being of children. Keep in mind that boys and girls are active for different reasons than adults, and place a high priority on education, motivation, and having fun. Remember also that participation in an after-school youth activity program is a personal choice, and that if children are unable to perform the activities or simply think the class is boring, it is unlikely they will continue to participate.

Instead of focusing on the outcomes of physical fitness training, teach children how to be physically active. Be enthusiastic about your job and show a genuine interest and concern for every child in your program, particularly those who are overweight, sedentary, or have physical or mental disabilities. With age-appropriate guidance and instruction, all children can condition their muscles and develop a positive attitude toward strength-building activities. When children have fun, experience success, and develop positive relationships with the instructor, they are more likely to continue participating.

Have regular conversations with the children in your program so you can listen to their concerns and make sensible recommendations as well as appropriate adjustments. Remember, along with your primary objective of creating a safe and enjoyable physical-activity program, you are also responsible for class management, quality instruction, and skill development. Successful youth strength training programs require preparation, coordination, and knowledgeable instruction.

The following guidelines can lead to high attendance and continued participation in a youth strength-training program.

1. Hire the best youth fitness instructors. To ensure a quality program, hire instructors who understand the physical and psychosocial uniqueness of youth. It is paramount to hire instructors who are good role models and who enjoy working with children.

2. Create an original name for your program. A name that projects a positive, healthy image that is appealing to children and their parents will help to promote your program.

3. Designate an area just for kids. An aesthetically pleasing environment with youth equipment and colorful posters will make children feel special and show others your true commitment to youth fitness.

4. Screen all participants. Parents should complete a medical history questionnaire for each child in the program. Some children, such as those with diabetes or a pre-existing orthopedic injury, may need approval from a physician prior to participation.

5. Meet and greet. Before the class officially starts, spend a few minutes getting to know the children in your program. Ask them about their day and show genuine interest and concern about topics they want to talk about.

6. Educate parents. Invite parents to observe your class and participate in free information sessions during after-school hours. Parents who understand the value of regular physical activity are more likely to encourage their children to participate in youth fitness programs and may themselves become more active.

7. Vary games and activities. Children will get bored if they perform the same games and activities during every class. Play different games and add new strength-training exercises to the program when appropriate.

8. Enforce program rules. You are responsible for enforcing program rules and proper behavior. Take a few minutes before every class to review program rules and consequences for unruly behavior.

9. Record progress. Teach children how to record their progress on workout cards. This will help to focus each child's attention on their own strength gains and improvements.

10. Experience success. Children who see themselves getting stronger will be more likely to stick with the program. Experiencing success, along with making friends and having fun, will contribute to enjoyment of, and participation in, the strength-training program.

Program Design

The strength-training programs in this chapter are designed for preadolescent boys and girls. Each strength-training program consists of a 15-minute introduction and general warm-up, 20 to 30 minutes of strength training, and a 15-minute period of games and cool-down activities. Children should participate in strength-building activities twice per week on nonconsecutive days. You can follow the youth strength-training programs described in this chapter, or modify the programs to meet the needs and abilities of children in your class.

Phase One: Introduction and Warm-up

Meet and greet the children and their parents in a convenient location. Get to know the children in your program and take the time to learn every child's name. Begin the first day of the program with a name game so the instructors and children can get to know each other. This helps break the ice and gets all the children talking and involved in group activities. This introductory period also serves as a transition to more formal warm-up activities, which include aerobic drills, obstacle courses, and flexibility exercises.

Encourage participants to create their own warm-up exercises and share ideas with the class. Many children enjoy dynamic warm-up activities (e.g., skipping, hopping, jumping) interspersed with recovery periods as needed. Since children do not normally engage in prolonged periods of aerobic exercise, an interval-type warm-up is more enjoyable and more consistent with how children play. Regardless of what type of activity is used during the warm-up period, focus on all the major muscle groups that will be used in the strength-training phase.

Phase Two: Strength Training

During this phase, children participate in a supervised program that is consistent with their needs and abilities. This is particularly important during the first few sessions when some children may be tempted to see how much weight they can lift. In this case, you may need to redirect children's energy and enthusiasm for strength training toward the development of proper exercise technique. It is always better to underestimate a child's strength and progress gradually, than start with heavy weights and risk an injury.

Begin every class with a review of safe training procedures and pay particular attention to teaching proper exercise technique. Most children have never strength trained before so take the time to teach children how to change the seat height on a weight machine or how to hold a dumbbell properly. Use "show and tell" demonstrations to assist in explaining proper exercise technique and encourage children to ask questions. Throughout the program, provide each child with constructive feedback and encouragement.

As children continue to strength train, their fitness levels will improve and they will gain confidence in their abilities to perform strength exercises properly. Over time, they will be able to complete the strength-training circuit in a shorter period of time. Thus, to continually provide a challenging training stimulus, gradually increase the repetitions, training weightloads, number of sets, or number of exercises. While children may perform eight exercises during the first week of the program, they may be able to complete 12 exercises in the same period of time following six to eight weeks of training.

Although different modes of training can be used to safely and effectively enhance the muscular fitness of preadolescent youth, three productive youth strength-training programs are featured here that use weight machines, free weights, or medicine balls and elastic bands, as described below. Note that bodyweight exercises for the abdominal and lower-back muscle groups are included in the weight-machine and free-weight programs for muscle balance and general conditioning. Of course, there is nothing wrong with a workout that combines different modes of strength training.

Phase Three: Games and Cool-down Activities

Complete the exercise session with games and activities that have moderate skill requirements. To maintain interest, structure the cool-down differently than the warm-up. Begin with a fun game that all of the children can play, and include cooperative games with parachutes or balloons so all of children have an opportunity to play together rather than compete against each other. After the games, quiet things down with cool-down calisthenics and stretching. Try to incorporate a variety of movements and positions—standing, sitting, or laying down—to stretch the body in different postures. Stretching can be made more enjoyable if children hold a ball or a stick while moving their body in different positions.

Summary

Two essential components of a successful youth strength-training program are competent instruction and gradual progression. Take the time to teach children how to strength train properly and focus on the development of proper form and technique on a variety of exercises. When appropriate, make the strength-training program more challenging by changing the training weight, number of sets, or choice of exercises. Remember that different modes of strength training have proven to be safe and effective for children, and there is not one program that is optimal for everyone. Lastly, do not overlook the importance of providing children in your program with a fun and rewarding experience that sparks a lifelong interest in physical activity.

O

obstacle course, 87

1 RM weightload, 20
  repetitions and number of performed, 21

osteoporosis, 4

overtraining, 24

overuse injuries, 6

overweight youth, pyschosocial benefits of
  strength training, 4–5

P

parent involvement, 86

partner twist, with medicine ball, 74

performance feedback, 78–79

physician approval, 86

plateaus, 11

positive feedback, 79

positive reinforcement, 79, 83

posture, 25, 26

program design, 85–89
  cool-down, 82, 87
  educational emphasis, 82–83
  games, 87
  introductory sessions, 80–81, 87
  variation, 11
  warm-up, 81, 87

program name, 86

progression, gradual, 26, 80

progressive overload, 10

progressive warm-up sets, 24

psychosocial health, 5

pullover, with medicine ball, 71

pull-ups, 3, 15

push, with medicine ball, 70

push-up, 3, 15, 56

Q

question-and-answer techniques, 80

R

range, strength training, 25, 26

records, 12, 87

reinforcement, 80

relaxation exercises, 82

repetitions, 21, 26, 88

resistance level, 20–21, 26

role modeling, 13, 86

rotary exercises, 25

rules, 87

running, 81

S

safety, 80

safety checklist, 12

SAID principle (Specific Adaptations to
  Imposed Demands), 10

seated dip, child-sized resistance
  machine, 43

seated row
  adult-sized resistance machine, 31
  with elastic band, 62

seated shoulder press, with elastic band, 63

self-esteem, 5

sets, 22–24, 26, 88

shoulder press
  adult-sized resistance machine, 32
  child-sized resistance machine, 41
  dumbbell, 48
  with medicine ball, 19
  seated, with elastic band, 63

show and tell demonstrations, 88

Y

American Academy of Pediatrics (2001). Strength training by children and adolescents. *Pediatrics,* 107, 1470–1472.

American Orthopaedic Society for Sports Medicine (1988). *Proceedings of the conference on strength training and the prepubescent.* Chicago: American Orthopaedic Society for Sports Medicine.

DeLorme, T. & Watkins, A. (1948). Techniques of progressive resistance exercise. *Archives of Physical Medicine,* 29, 263–273.

Faigenbaum, A. (2003). Youth resistance training. *President's Council on Physical Fitness and Sports Research Digest,* 4, 3, 1–8.

Faigenbaum, A. (2001). Strength training and children's health. *Journal of Physical Education Recreation and Dance,* 72, 3, 24–30.

Faigenbaum, A. (2000). Strength training for children and adolescents. *Clinics in Sports Medicine,* 19, 593–619.

Faigenbaum, A. (1995). Psychosocial benefits of prepubescent strength training. *Strength and Conditioning,* 17, 28–32.

Faigenbaum, A. et al. (2002). Comparison of 1 day and 2 days per week of strength training in children. *Research Quarterly for Exercise and Sport,* 73, 416–424.

Faigenbaum, A. et al. (2001). The effects of different resistance training protocols on upper body strength and endurance development in children. *Journal of Strength and Conditioning Research,* 15, 4, 459–465.

Faigenbaum, A. et al. (1999). The effects of different resistance training protocols on muscular strength and endurance development in children. *Pediatrics,* 104, 1, e5.

Faigenbaum, A. et al. (1996a). Youth resistance training: Position statement paper and literature review. *Strength and Conditioning,* 18, 62–75.

Faigenbaum, A. et al. (1996b). The effects of strength training and detraining on children. *Journal of Strength and Conditioning Research,* 10, 109–114.

Faigenbaum, A. et al. (1993). The effects of a twice per week strength training program on children. *Pediatric Exercise Science,* 5, 339–346.

Faigenbaum, A. & Schram, J. (2004). Can resistance training reduce injuries in youth sports? *Strength and Conditioning Journal,* 26, 3, 16–21.

Faigenbaum, A. & Westcott, W. (2001). *Youth Fitness.* San Diego, Calif.: American Council on Exercise.

Faigenbaum, A & Westcott, W. (2000). *Strength and Power Training for Young Athletes.* Champaign, Ill.: Human Kinetics Publishers.

Falk, B., & Tenenbaum, G. (1996). The effectiveness of resistance training in children: A meta-analysis. *Sports Medicine,* 22, 176–186.

Flegal, K. (1999). The obesity epidemic in children and adults: Current evidence and research issues. *Medicine and Science in Sports and Exercise,* 31, 11, S509–S514.

Gullich, A. & Schmidtbleicher, D. (1996). MVC-induced short-term potentiation of explosive force. *New Studies in Athletics,* 11, 67–81.

Hamill, B. (1994). Relative safety of weight lifting and weight training. *Journal of Strength and Conditioning Research,* 8, 53–57.

Heidt, R. (2000). Avoidance of soccer injuries with preseason conditioning. *American Journal of Sports Medicine,* 28, 659–662.

Hewett, T. et al. (1999). The effect of neuromuscular training on the incidence of knee injury in female athletes. *American Journal of Sports Medicine,* 27, 699–705.

Holloway, J. et al. (1988). Self-efficacy and training in adolescent girls. *Journal of Applied Social Psychology,* 18, 699–719.

Kato, S. & Ishiko, T. (1964). Obstructed growth of children's bones due to excessive labor in remote corners, In: Kato, S. (Ed): *Proceedings of the International Congress of Sports Sciences.* Tokyo: Japanese Union of Sport Sciences.

LaRosa Loud, R. (1999). Take some of the work out of kids' workout. *Perspective,* 25, 34–37.

Lillegard, W. et al. (1997). Efficacy of strength training in prepubescent to early postpubescent males and females: Effects of gender and maturity. *Pediatric Rehabilitation,* 1, 147–157.

Mediate, P. & Faigenbaum, A. (2004). *Medicine Ball Training for All.* Monterey, Calif.: Healthy Learning.

Morris, F. et al. (1997). Prospective ten month exercise intervention in premenarcheal girls: Positive effects on bone and lean mass. *Journal of Bone and Mineral Research,* 12, 1453–1462.

Sadres, E. et al. (2001). The effect of long-term resistance training on anthropometric measures, muscle strength, and self concept in pre-pubertal boys. *Pediatric Exercise Science,* 13, 357–372.

Smith, A., Andrish, J., & Micheli, L. (1993). The prevention of sports injuries on children and adolescents. *Medicine and Science in Sports and Exercise,* S25, 1–7.

U.S. Department of Health and Human Services. *Physical Activity and Health: A Report from the Surgeon General.* (1996). Atlanta, GA: U.S. Department of Health and Human Services, Centers for Disease Control and Prevention, National Center for Chronic Disease Prevention and Health Promotion.

Vincent, S. et al. (2003). Activity levels and body mass index of children in the United States, Sweden and Australia. *Medicine and Science in Sports and Exercise,* 35, 8, 1367–1373.

Weiss, M. (2000). Motivating kids in physical activity. *President's Council on Physical Fitness and Sports Research*

Digest, 3, 11, 1–8.

Weltman, A. et al. (1986). The effects of hydraulic resistance strength training in pre-pubertal males. *Medicine and Science in Sports and Exercise,* 18, 629–638.

Westcott, W. (2000). Strength training frequency. *Fitness Management,* 16, 12, 50–54.

Westcott, W. (1991). Role model instructors. *Fitness Management,* 7, 4, 48–50.

Westcott, W. et al. (2003). Using performance feedback in strength training. *Fitness Management,* 19, 10, 28–33.

Westcott, W. & Faigenbaum, A. (2003). Strength training for kids. *IDEA Health and Fitness Source,* 21, 4, 36–43.

Westcott, W. & Faigenbaum, A. (2001). Sensible strength training for preadolescents. *Fitness Management,* 17, 6, 28–30.

Westcott, W. & Faigenbaum, A. (1998). Sensible strength training during youth. *IDEA Health and Fitness Source,* 16, 32–39.

Westcott, W., Tolken, J., & Wessner, B. (1995). School-based conditioning programs for physically unfit children. *Strength and Conditioning,* 17, 5–9.

Williams, D. (1991). The effect of weight training on performance in selected motor activities for preadolescent males. *Journal of Applied Sports Science Research.* 5:170.

Young, W. & Behm, D. (2003). Effects of running, static stretching and practice jumps on explosive force production and jumping performance. *Journal of Sports Medicine and Physical Fitness,* 43, 21–27.

Zwiren, L.D. (2001). Exercise testing and prescription considerations throughout childhood. In: *ACSM's Resource Manual for Guidelines for Exercise Testing and Prescription* (4th ed.). New York: Lippincott Williams & Wilkins.

ABOUT THE AUTHORS

Avery D. Faigenbaum, Ed.D., is an associate professor in the Department of Health and Exercise Science at The College of New Jersey in Ewing, New Jersey. He is a leading researcher and practitioner in the area of youth strength training and lectures across the country to fitness and sports medicine organizations. Dr. Faigenbaum is a Fellow of the American College of Sports Medicine and currently serves on the Board of Directors of the National Strength and Conditioning Association.

Wayne L. Westcott, Ph.D., is the fitness research director at the South Shore YMCA in Quincy, Massachusetts. He is recognized as a leading authority on fitness and has served as a strength training consultant for numerous professional organizations, including the President's Council on Physical Fitness and Sports, American Council on Exercise, the YMCA of the USA, and the United States Navy. Dr. Westcott has authored 20 books on strength training and published more than 400 articles in professional journals.